Zen and the Art of Persuasive Writing

HON. DAVID D. WEINZWEIG

AMERICAN BAR ASSOCIATION

Cover design by Elizabeth Kulak/ABA Design

Printed in the United States of America.

29 28 27 26 25   5 4 3 2 1

A catalog record for this book is available from the Library of Congress.

Discounts are available for books ordered in bulk. Special consideration is given to state bars, CLE programs, and other bar-related organizations. Inquire at Book Publishing, ABA Publishing, American Bar Association, 321 N. Clark Street, Chicago, Illinois 60654-7598.

www.shopABA.org

To my family.

Most books about writing
are filled with bullshit.

—STEPHEN KING[1]

TABLE OF CONTENTS

FOREWORD ix
ABOUT THE AUTHOR xiii
INTRODUCTION xv
THE MANTRAS xxi
CHAPTER 1 BE AWARE OF THE AUDIENCE 1
§ 1 Absent Readers and Absent Writers 1
§ 2 Know and Motivate the Reader 5
§ 3 The Reader's Brain 7
§ 4 The Judge's Brain 12
CHAPTER 2 BE LESS CATEGORICAL 21
CHAPTER 3 BE CLEAR AND CONCRETE 23
§ 1 Opacity Is a Vice, Clarity Is a Virtue 24
§ 2 Reasons for Unclear and Abstract Writing 29
§ 3 Fallout of Fuzzy Writing 35
§ 4 Mindful Word Choice 40
§ 5 Mindful Grammar 89
§ 6 Distrust Abstract Words and Phrases 111
§ 7 Distrust Abstract Grammar 117
§ 8 Abstract Things 129
§ 9 Hemingway and Orwell, Not Faulkner 142

Chapter 4 BE CONCISE 147

§ 1 Reasons for Prolixity 149

§ 2 Keep It Tight 152

§ 3 Less Is More 154

§ 4 Hard Work 157

§ 5 Omit Needless Words 159

Chapter 5 BE COHESIVE AND COHERENT 171

§ 1 Cohesion 172

§ 2 Coherence 180

Chapter 6 BE COMPELLING 199

§ 1 Persuasion 199

§ 2 Impactful Introductions 201

§ 3 A Compelling Narrative 211

§ 4 Make Your Writing Inviting 215

§ 5 Mindful Citation 231

§ 6 Mindful Footnotes 234

§ 7 Mindful Block Quotes 235

§ 8 Mindful Lists 236

§ 9 Mindful Punctuation 237

§ 10 Mindful Typography 250

CHAPTER 7 BE CREDIBLE 251

§ 1 Honest 252

§ 2 Connect and Concede 254

§ 3 Accurate and Responsive 255

§ 4 Respectful 256

CHAPTER 8 BE A READER AND WRITER 259

§ 1 Read More 259

§ 2 Write More 261

CHAPTER 9 BE METICULOUS AND REWRITE 263

§ 1 Structure 265

§ 2 Length 267

§ 3 Clarity 269

§ 4 Accuracy and Typos 271

§ 5 Feedback 273

CHAPTER 10 CONCLUSION 277

ACKNOWLEDGMENTS 281

TRANSITION CHEAT SHEET APPX I 283

ONE WORD IS OFTEN ENOUGH APPX II 287

ANSWERS TO QUESTIONS APPX III 291

ENDNOTES 307

FOREWORD

Almost 75 years have passed since Eugen Herrigel introduced the West to Eastern spirituality with his 92-page classic, *Zen in the Art of Archery*, where Herrigel recounted his five-year spiritual retreat to Japan.

It was 1924. Herrigel jumped at the chance to teach philosophy at Tokyo Imperial University, yearning to explore his second passion—Zen Buddhism. Herrigel had long been smitten by Zen Buddhism, and he wanted to learn more. Japan offered that chance. Zen had been practiced and preached there for nearly 1,500 years. Even better, the gig would not require much work because Herrigel taught the same class to German students at a university near Nuremberg.

So Herrigel and his wife packed their bags and traveled to Tokyo where Herrigel set out to find a proper Zen master to guide his spiritual journey. But no master wanted him. "Never yet," Herrigel was told, "had any European seriously concerned himself with Zen," and "it was quite hopeless for a European to attempt to penetrate into this realm of spiritual life."[2]

Despondent but not defeated, Herrigel was encouraged to start elsewhere by learning the teachings of Japanese arts associated with the Zen gospel, a diverse range of hobbies from archery to flower arrangements. He picked archery, enrolling in a five-year program under the tutelage of an archery master.

All was not lost. Herrigel improved his archery shot and learned lots about Eastern spirituality. And he used that experience to author the best-selling book *Zen in the Art of Archery*, sparking a new genre and paving the way for 200 or so books and titles with similar names and themes, including *Zen and the Art of Motorcycle Maintenance* (1974) and *Zen and the Art of Competitive Eating* (2004).

That leads us here. Why did I name this book *Zen and the Art of Persuasive Writing*? Two reasons:

First, persuasive writing *is* an art. Justice Ruth Bader Ginsburg said so. She once told Bryan Garner, "[l]aw should be a literary profession, and the best legal practitioners regard law as an art as well as a craft."[3] We explore the art and craft of persuasive writing in these pages.

Second, Zen has much to teach us about writing and persuasive writing. Great writers are mindful writers, and mindful writers remember their readers, ever aware of the reading brain's needs and expectations.

Oh! I almost forgot. Eugen Herrigel—the original *Zen in the Art* author. Remember him? Well, after finishing his archery lessons in 1929, Herrigel returned to Germany and promptly rekindled his first passion—the Third Reich—joining Adolf Hitler just a decade before Germany invaded Poland to unleash World War II.

Don't act surprised. Just 14 years before Herrigel wrote *Zen in the Art of Archery*, he penned *The Task of Philosophy in the New Third Reich*. It just didn't generate the same enthusiasm across the pond.

ABOUT THE AUTHOR

DAVID D. WEINZWEIG is the Vice Chief Judge of the Arizona Court of Appeals, Division One. Before joining the court, Judge Weinzweig spent decades at the highest levels of government and private practice, specializing in constitutional law and antitrust law. He co-authored legal treatises on antitrust law, consumer protection and benchmarking. Since joining the court, Judge Weinzweig has authored thousands of orders, opinions and memorandum decisions. He teaches the art and science of persuasive writing to judges, lawyers, law clerks and law students across the nation.

INTRODUCTION

We have an epidemic. The virus is known to travel on paper and transmit over the keyboard: it jumps from old lawyer to young lawyer, preys on the inexperienced and insecure lawyer, and thrives in the imprecise and indifferent lawyer. It spreads like wildfire in college towns and institutions of higher learning. And it mutates! Oh boy, does it mutate. Turning verbs into nouns. Adverbs flourish. Adjectives and jargon run free.

That epidemic is bad writing—especially legal and persuasive writing. Legal prose is often dull and opaque, redundant and bumpy, labored and disorganized. It sputters and coughs in the opening sentences, leaving an unnavigable and incomprehensible mess for the reader to withstand. It's hard to read, harder to understand and hardest to remember. It prefers abstractions—abstract words and abstract grammar; abstract facts and abstract arguments. And it weighs on the reader's brain.

Why is so much legal and persuasive prose so bad? I think it's because many legal writers never stop to think about their readers. The elixir for this oversight is mindfulness. A persuasive writer anticipates, meets and remembers the preferences and expectations of his readers. He cares about communication and seizes control of his literary fate—guiding the writing process from start to finish. He knows why he writes, what he writes and how he writes. He knows that persuasive prose is not a monologue, but a dialogue between writer and reader. This book introduces the path to persuasion in nine mantras.

Be aware of the audience. A persuasive writer understands the singular importance of the audience and appreciates the inherent challenges that arise when time and distance separate readers from writers, so he channels the readers to anticipate and answer their questions.

Be less categorical. Persuasive writers know that few rules are absolute. When it comes to persuasion, musty preferences are not nimble enough to track the dynamic evolution of language and communication.

Be clear and concrete. Persuasive prose conveys hard facts and ideas in plain and simple words. It favors plain nouns and vivid verbs; disfavors jargon and abstractions. It flows and sounds natural, even conversational, never driving readers to secondary sources to sharpen an image or understand a point. A persuasive writer appeals to the human senses, knowing that abstractions extract a heavy cognitive toll on the reader's brain. He knows the law has clung to abstract grammar and abstract words for hundreds of years, but he forsakes obtuse writing in the name of communication.

Be concise. A persuasive writer severs the meaningful from the meaningless. He is focused and assured. He understands the nuances of his argument—its strengths and weaknesses—and he uses that knowledge to disentangle the issues and unscramble the facts.

Be cohesive and coherent. Persuasive prose is easy on the eyes and simple to navigate, wielding the power of transitions and priming. A persuasive writer knows how his document fits together, sentence to sentence and paragraph to paragraph.

Be compelling. A persuasive writer holds the readers' attention and interest for long enough to move their hearts and minds. He knows that persuasive prose is art, both literary and logical, and uses the power of analogy and literary devices to that end.

Be credible. A persuasive writer earns his reputation with colleagues and the courts, acting honestly and urging only plausible arguments with clarity of thought. A fine reputation is not purchased or invoked by the advocate; rather, it is bestowed by the audience.

Be a reader and writer. A persuasive writer reads and reverse-engineers the language, style and approach of the stuff he likes. He knows what moves him and leverages that experience to improve his writing. He writes frequently to cultivate and refine his skills.

Be meticulous and rewrite. A persuasive writer labors to guarantee the audience will understand his point. He knows that persuasive prose is the end product of many drafts and myriad decisions. A persuasive writer sheds any stubborn, unproductive attachment to his own words and thoughts—like a rattlesnake sheds its skin. He drafts and redrafts until it flows.

When writers account for these nine mantras, persuasive prose is sublime. It leaps from the page and grabs readers by the collar, commanding their interest and attention until the very last word.

A word about my approach and teaching style. We immerse ourselves in the fundamentals of writing and explore the art of persuasion from the reader's perspective. My tools are practical, my lessons universal, presented for immediate use and instant improvement. In the words of our founding father Thomas Paine, "I offer nothing more than simple facts, plain arguments, and common sense."[4]

My advice is anchored in science because writing is an intensely personal exercise. When someone audits our words, it causes our stomachs to squirm, our blood pressure to increase, and our brows to furrow, activating an arsenal of defense mechanisms. By adding an objective element to persuasive writing—data from studies in psychology and psycholinguistics—I hope to overcome this natural reaction. Even better, the book is peppered with research that validates what I teach.

This book is not about hard and fast rules. My hope is to deliver practical advice in an accessible and entertaining way. You may read the pages and chapters in any order, picking the advice that resonates with you.

I lean on history's best and brightest to model and confirm my methods. My guest luminaries are a motley crew of founding fathers and philosophers, authors and scientists. Each has left us his or her enduring wisdom on language and literature, which I cherish and think you will too, delivered with humor and grace.

My guest luminaries have much to teach about the art of legal and persuasive writing. From Mark Twain, a preference for concrete prose and command of modern English. From William Shakespeare, a love of concision. From Ernest Hemingway, a predatory instinct to eliminate unnecessary words and trifling points. From the Rolling Stones, a mistrust of convention. From Stephen King, a fidelity to nouns and verbs and intolerance for adverbs and adjectives. The plain and simple words of these luminaries are sprinkled throughout this book.

When it comes to legal writers, I rely on the wisdom and punchy prose of great advocates—the lions of our profession. I extract jurisprudential nectar from past and present justices and judges. You have your favorites; I have mine. From the past, I cherish Antonin Scalia, Learned Hand and Robert Jackson. From the present, I admire Richard Posner and Elena Kagan. Their helpful advice fuels lucid prose. I include some of my stuff too, spanning years of private practice, government counsel and now the bench.

Legal writing is the common thread that binds all forms of law practice. Many law students see legal writing class as an elective, unworthy of their finite attention because it's not substantive law. That's wrong. A lawyer who cannot write well is like an opera singer with laryngitis.

Meditation

THE MANTRAS

Chapter 1 Be Aware of the Audience
Chapter 2 Be Less Categorical
Chapter 3 Be Clear and Concrete
Chapter 4 Be Concise
Chapter 5 Be Cohesive and Coherent
Chapter 6 Be Compelling
Chapter 7 Be Credible
Chapter 8 Be a Reader and Writer
Chapter 9 Be Meticulous and Rewrite

What is persuasive prose? When asked that question, I think of Justice Potter Stewart's concurrence in *Jacobellis v. Ohio,* 378 U.S. 184 (1964). You know the case. Mr. Jacobellis presented an erotic French film called *Les Amants* at a movie theater in Ohio. On that basis, he was charged with and convicted of "possessing and exhibiting an obscene film" under Ohio law. His appeal eventually reached the United States Supreme Court, which pronounced the movie was not obscene and reversed his conviction.

Justice Stewart wrote separately to describe the futile task of defining hardcore pornography. He wrote, "I shall not today attempt further to define [hardcore pornography], and perhaps I could never succeed in intelligibly doing so. But I know it when I see it, and the motion picture involved in this case is not that."

That's how I know persuasive prose—I know it when I read it. The good stuff is clear and concise, plain and concrete. And it hums, offering a pleasant rhythm. The bad stuff is dense and abstract, ornate and bloated. And it's coarse, endured without joy or interest.

But those are mere adjectives, and you will learn that adjectives were not invented to impart practical direction. For a practical definition of persuasive prose, let's turn to the mantras.

CHAPTER 1
BE AWARE OF THE AUDIENCE

1 ABSENT READERS AND ABSENT WRITERS
2 KNOW AND MOTIVATE THE READER
3 THE READER'S BRAIN
4 THE JUDGE'S BRAIN

§ 1 Absent Readers and Absent Writers

The single biggest problem in communication is the illusion that it has taken place.

—GEORGE BERNARD SHAW[5]

Ancient Mesopotamians used pictures of basic objects to preserve and describe their culture. The Phoenicians pivoted from pictures to symbols around 1600 B.C., a harbinger of our modern alphabet. Each symbol represented a spoken sound, but the reader read the symbols from right to left.

This method spread to Israel and Greece, where the Phoenician alphabet was refashioned into the Greek alphabet, but the Greeks invented vowels and redirected the reader from left to right.

The Romans then used the Greek alphabet to make the Latin alphabet, and hundreds of languages have sprung from the Latin alphabet, including English.

When the Phoenicians invented the alphabet and written communication, they invented a method to exchange and preserve thought—long after the thinker has stopped thinking. Words live on the page, where they reverberate beyond our physical and temporal reach. A device that teleports ideas through space and time. Yes, it sounds like *Star Wars*, but I only mean to say that shouting distance was no longer required to make a point. As a result, we can read the Gettysburg Address in 2024, even though President Abraham Lincoln died in April 1865. Lincoln understood this power and described it well:

> *Writing, the art of communicating*
> *thoughts to the mind through the eye,*
> *is the great invention of the world[,]*
> *enabling us to converse with the*
> *dead, the absent, and the unborn,*
> *at all distances of time and space.*
>
> —Abraham Lincoln[6]

But it's not all sunshine and rainbows. The distance of time and space between readers and writers produced new challenges, which I call the **Absent Reader** and the **Absent Writer.**

An absent reader for the writer.

First, a writer writes alone. Readers are absent when writers craft and recraft their words and sentences. The reader is not in the room during the creative process, peering over the writer's shoulder to ask questions and raise concerns:

What does this mean?
Why are you discussing that point?
I'm losing interest.
OK bruh, I'm lost.

And because the reader is absent, writers cannot deploy their innate communication skills—that empathetic reflex hardwired into the human brain over thousands of years. When humans speak face-to-face, the speaker can read and react. He might change words or tone based on the listener's facial expressions and body language—a nod from the listener and the speaker continues forward; a blank stare and the speaker revisits the point. Not so when writing.

An absent writer for the reader.

Second, a reader reads alone. Writers are absent when readers read and process their words and sentences. A reader may need guidance, but the writer is not present in real time to field questions:

When I wrote this, I meant that.
I'm discussing this point because of that.
This point is related to that point.
You might be lost because I forgot
to tell you something.

A mindful writer knows he no longer controls how a message is delivered once his words and sentences are released into the ether. For that reason, he crafts from the perspective of his readers, anticipating their wants and needs.

> *I think there is writing genius as well—which consists primarily of the ability to place oneself in the shoes of one's audience. To assume only what they assume; to anticipate what they anticipate; to explain what they need explained; to think what they must be thinking; to feel what they must be feeling.*
>
> —Justice Antonin Scalia[7]

§ 2 *Know and Motivate the Reader*

It is the hearer that determines
the speech's end and object.

—Aristotle[8]

To overcome and even exploit the distance between reader and writer, persuasive writers toil to understand their readers. Each reader consumes information through a different lens, customized by their background, knowledge and experience. A persuasive writer calibrates and fine tunes his approach to meet that reader's unique expectations.

Persuasive writers use their life and professional experience, along with their pre-programmed communication instincts, to draft with prescience and intention. They anticipate and answer reader questions before they are ever posed, spotting the points or arguments most likely to confuse or overwhelm the readers, and easing the path to comprehension.

It's not like you're incapable of thinking like a reader. You are one! In fact, you're reading right now. So use that inside advantage to your benefit. Write to others as you would have others write to you.

Meditation

Picture the readers and write for them. Ask around. You might not have met your reader personally, but you can find readers with similar backgrounds, values and interests. Test drive your argument and narrative with them. Look for their reaction. What motivates them? What persuades them? What must they know to understand the next paragraph? It's like Carnac the Magnificent or a mentalist routine in Las Vegas.

Persuasive and legal writing have a long and diverse bench of readers who fall into one of three groups—judges, lawyers and non-lawyers. Each member of each group, however, shares at least one thing in common. All readers have a brain! Persuasive prose accounts for the frailties of the human brain.

> Your message and approach are influenced if not directed by your audience.
>
> *Meditation*

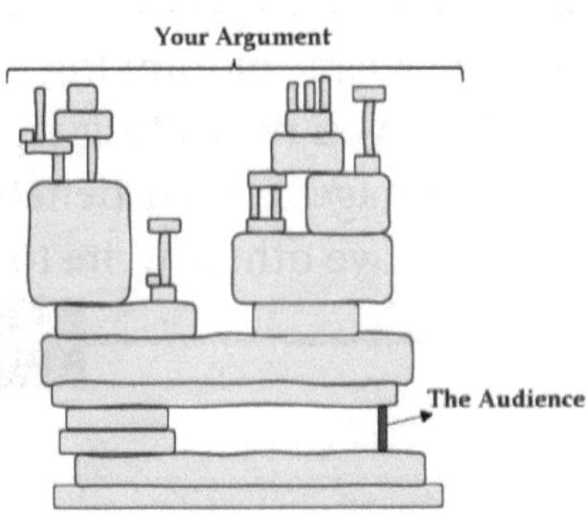

§ 3 *The Reader's Brain*

A. Reading Taxes the Brain

Reading is hard on the brain. To read text, the reader must engage and coordinate distinct, complex cognitive functions located in distinct parts of the brain, including the sensory and reasoning systems. Language and thought are processed by different regions of the brain.[9]

Readers must recognize words from prior encounters, decipher meaning, recall information, overcome ambiguity and merge new information into the world of old information. Readers assign roles to words in a sentence, and examine those words against other words in the sentence. This empowers the reader to anticipate how the sentence will play out, structurally.

And this weighs on the brain. The burden imposed on the human brain when reading is called **cognitive load**. Author and scholar Yellowlees Douglas explained why reading is so hard in *The Reader's Brain*. She explained that "[r]eading requires a substantial cognitive load merely in completing the process of identifying, predicting, and confirming."[10] Much of that load is handled by the prefrontal cortex because it welcomes and processes the abstract thought that infests academic and legal writing.[11]

The capacity of the prefrontal cortex is not infinite. When forced to read and reread the same words, sentences and paragraphs a second or third time, the reader has one foot out the door. These documents are hard to read and understand. As Ms. Douglas stressed: "Reading is only efficient when the process is looking forward, not bogged down in backtracking."[12] And eventually the brain hits tilt and the reader places the document aside.

It's hard to persuade an overwhelmed reader. Readers cannot be moved unless they understand your point. Persuasive writers thus labor with their prose to reduce the cognitive tax extracted from the reader's brain—making it readable.

B. How to Ease the Load?

From developments in psycholinguistics and cognitive psychology, we have a general sense of what readers want and do not want. Researchers have developed a rich body of data in these fields about how the human brain processes, manipulates and gains knowledge. We now know what kind of prose is most easily read, assimilated and recalled.

Thanks to neuroimaging technologies, we can peek under the cranial hood and watch how prose is read and processed. These technologies include functional magnetic resonance imaging (fMRI), magnetoencephalograms (MEGs), diffusion tensor imaging (DTIs), electroencephalograms (EEGs), positron emission tomography (PET scans) and rapid eye movement scans.

The best known is fMRI, which measures changes in brain metabolism over time. An MEG measures the magnetic fields produced by your brain's electrical currents; a DTI measures the diffusion of hydrogen in the brain; an EEG measures the electrical impulses discharged from the scalp; a PET scan shows blood flow as the brain processes information; and rapid eye movement scans track the reading eye's movement as it consumes text.

This book will explore the growing body of research, but here's a preview:

Concrete, not abstract. When presented in concrete words and concrete grammar, an argument is accessible—easily consumed and processed.[13] To that end, persuasive writers prefer plain words over ornate words, concrete images over abstract concepts, precise words over fuzzy words and concision over volume. We'll take a deep dive in Chapter 3.

> *If your writing is hard to understand, your reader will wind up confused, irritated or just plain bored. Reading your words will be harder and take longer, and there's a good chance that the reader will just give up. All this thought-crunching uses up brainpower, which increases what psychologists call cognitive load. The reader's brain can only do so much. If you give them too many things to think about at once, some of them will get squeezed out.*
>
> —Tom Albrighton[14]

Prime for cognitive ease. When readers encounter words and ideas they've read before, they feel cognitive ease. As discussed in Chapter 5 (Be Cohesive and Coherent) readers enjoy seeing things a second and third time. It's called priming. A primed idea looks familiar, sounds better and feels more natural. A primed idea is also more persuasive. American cognitive psychologist Larry Jacoby explained:

> The experience of familiarity has a simple but powerful quality of "pastness" that seems to indicate that it is a direct reflection of prior experience.[15]

Link words and ideas. Readers are swayed when writers link their words and ideas by logic, preferences and association. Words are linked to remind the reader of facts and arguments. Read more about this in Chapter 5.

Gain the reader's trust. An act of persuasion teeters on trust. Readers are open-minded and flexible when they read the words of a writer they trust. Gain a reader's trust to move his mind. Learn more on this in Chapter 7, Be Credible.

Present a fresh and concise offering. Vary the length of your sentences and paragraphs, and vary the level of detail. Discover more in Chapter 6, Be Compelling.

§ 4 *The Judge's Brain*

Know your judge. A judge's brain is often the difference between success or failure, so strive to understand your judge—her preferences and requirements, tendencies and expectations. To gain her attention, account for her perspective.

> *Think of how many dreary briefs a judge has to read in a judicial lifetime. What can you do to make your work sparkle, so that your judge actually looks forward to reading what you have to say?*
>
> —James W. McElhaney[16]

Most judges are generalists who are legally compelled to hear and resolve a diverse menu of issues in a broad universe of disputes. They might not immediately understand or appreciate the weight of a particular case or argument. So tell them—give them pause.

A. Motivation

What moves a judge? From my personal and professional experience, judges are motivated by similar things:

Respect for the judicial branch and the rule of law.	Judges hold the judiciary in high regard and bristle when it's disrespected. They are serious about the rule of law and displeased when it's forsaken.
New and expanded laws.	Judges are careful to honor their oath and constitutional job description. They don't aspire to create new laws or expand old ones.
Gravity.	Judges know the weight and reach of their decisions, and they want to get it right.
Avoiding reversal.	Most decisions are subject to review and reversible. Judges fear reversal because it relegates their hard work to the dustbin of history.
Fairness.	Judges want to be fair and reach the fairest conclusion under the law.

Judicial efficiency.	Judges want their dockets to move forward, dreading the never-ending lawsuit.
Jurisdiction.	Judges want to know their work will count and not be ignored for lack of jurisdiction.

Persuasive writers know what moves a judge and deploy that knowledge to frame their narrative and argument—aligning motivation and theory.

Enough about abstract motivations. Here are a handful of real-world appeals to those motivations:

Respect for the law. Avoiding reversal.	Defendant asks this court to depart from 140 years of binding precedent.
Gravity. New terrain. Avoiding reversal.	If this court accepts that argument, it will have declared 36 unrelated Arizona statutes unconstitutional.
New laws. Respect for the law.	Plaintiff refashions the requirements for relief, adding two steps that never appear in the statute.

Fairness. Gravity.	Pete Rand stole everything from 10 senior citizens, leaving them with no assets to buy food or medicine.
Efficiency. Respect for the law.	This relief, if granted, would damage the fabric of California tort law and inspire a flood of litigation.
Fairness. Gravity.	The Islamic Republic of Iran funded the murder of 241 Marines in 1983. This lawsuit seeks compensation for the family members of eight servicemen killed on that infamous day.
Jurisdiction.	Defendant lives and works in North Carolina, beyond the constitutional reach of this South Carolina court.

B. The Individual Judge

And yet, judges are unique. Each has preferences and tendencies. Each has a distinct decisional history. Persuasive writers account for those preferences and tendencies, and research that decisional history. Loads of resources are available for persuasive writers to learn about their individual judge.

Westlaw is great to learn about state and federal appellate court judges, along with federal district court judges. When assigned a judge or judges, read their cases. Limit your search to a particular judge with this connector:

JU(Weinzweig) and search query

With that query, the persuasive writer marshals a goldmine of information about the judge—what she has written, what persuades her and her judicial philosophy. A persuasive writer accounts for how an assigned judge describes the burden of proof or standard of review. Like all writers, judges are open to their own words and it's normally safe to parrot them back.

You might strike gold or strike out. An advocate may find the assigned judge has considered and decided the very issue in their lawsuit. Armed with that knowledge, the persuasive writer handcrafts the narrative and argument most likely to move the audience.

More work is required to learn about state trial court judges, but some of their decisions are available on Westlaw. Read their biographies online. Read articles written by or about them. Watch their oral arguments.

Ask colleagues. Approach the lawyers inside and outside your group. Ask them, what works with this judge? What doesn't work with that judge? What irritates this judge? What moves that judge?

To gain a competitive edge, some government agencies and many law firms leverage their institutional knowledge in the cloud, accumulating a central repository for information about state and federal court judges. Attorneys at these agencies and businesses have easy access to this library. From my experience, the repository has decisions, forms, news articles and memoranda from attorneys who appear before the judge.

If you're paid to move hearts and minds, then your profit or success often depends on judges. Work to understand their needs, preferences, tendencies, individual practices, expectations and judicial philosophies.

C. Court, Procedural Posture and Standard of Review

Persuasive writers also account for the level of court and judge. To persuade a judge at any level, you must understand and appreciate their function and where they come from:

- Trial court judges are often required to make findings of fact and conclusions of law. They are happy when writers help finish that task.
- Appellate judges are less interested in emotion and reticent to revisit a trial court's factual findings.

Don't forget the procedure posture and court rules. A Rule 12(b) motion is disfavored because it's filed before the parties conduct any discovery. That motion is only successful when the defect is unfixable. A Rule 56 motion will not succeed unless the record has no disputed material issues of fact. Study the dueling statements of fact to leverage uncontested points and factual concessions. Heed the record on appeal.

And don't forget the standard of review. Not all judicial review is plenary. The standard of review affects how and what you write. Writers must account for the standard of review when choosing their facts and crafting their arguments. Review is broad but circumscribed on fact issues, and broadest on issues of interpretation and questions of law.

Consult this cheat sheet when crafting your argument on appeal:

De novo? *Less interested* in the trial court's reasoning and *less deferential* to its fact findings. This is the standard of review for motions to dismiss, summary judgment, conclusions of law and legal interpretations, including interpretations of constitutions, statutes and contracts.

Abuse of discretion? *More interested* in the trial court's reasoning and *more deferential* to its fact finding. This standard of review is used for evidentiary rulings, motions to amend and findings of fact.

Chapter 2
BE LESS CATEGORICAL

Writing rules are everywhere—in every profession, every law firm, and every government agency. Countless books have been authored with categorical rules, but language is not a commodity and one approach does not fit all. If you're coming here for absolute rules, you'll leave empty-handed. My only cause is that of communication. My only rule is to account for the readers—their wants and needs. When convention reigns supreme, content and quality may suffer.

The Simpsons has supplied great advice for most things in life and the rules of persuasive writing are no exception. To illustrate our second mantra, I'll borrow a line from Mick Jagger's character in *The Simpsons*. Classic episode: Mick and Keith Richards star as owners of their very own rock-and-roll fantasy camp. Early in the episode, the pair appear from nowhere and Mick riles up the campers with opening remarks to kick things off:

> Welcome to rock and roll fantasy camp, where you'll experience the complete rock and roll lifestyle—without the lawsuits and

> STDs. So get a good night sleep, and remember—Rule number one: There are no rules![17] Rule number two: No outside food.

Persuasive writers know that few rules are absolute. When it comes to persuasion, they are more concerned about reader comprehension than being faithful to musty, historical preferences. This stamp will alert you to exceptions of so-called absolute rules.

Chapter 3
BE CLEAR AND CONCRETE

1 Opacity Is a Vice, Clarity Is a Virtue
2 Reasons for Unclear and Abstract Writing
3 Fallout of Fuzzy Writing
4 Mindful Word Choice
5 Mindful Grammar
6 Distrust Abstract Words and Phrases
7 Distrust Abstract Grammar
8 Abstract Things
9 Hemingway and Orwell, Not Faulkner

Clarity is your first duty because without it the listener cannot even offer you that most elementary of courtesies, the honor of disagreement.

—R.N.S. Topping[18]

§ 1 Opacity Is a Vice, Clarity Is a Virtue

Clarity is a cardinal courtesy paid by writers to readers. Justice Ruth Bader Ginsburg placed a premium on clear language. She told her clerks, "the goal is to write an opinion where no sentence should need to be read twice."[19] To accomplish this goal, Justice Ginsburg went through "innumerable drafts" to prune her opinions of abstractions.[20] I share her reverence for clarity.

A. What Is Clear Writing?

Clear writers take a plain and lucid approach to writing because it eases understanding and relieves the reading brain. They are convinced that readers must never be compelled to consult dictionary.com to understand an argument or forced to read the same sentence and paragraph more than once.

Think of a play-by-play announcer who calls sports on the radio. Clarity is paramount for them to recount the action. Announcers must describe each goal or pass or foul as observed by their mind's eye—all in plain and simple words that listeners can immediately see and grasp:

The Knicks jump out to a quick lead of 11 to nothing.

Jalen Brunson gets the ball at the top of the key. Players from both teams are bunched under the hoop.

Brunson looks to his right and his left and then drives to the hoop for a slam dunk. The lead balloons to 13.

Clear writers want their readers to read and process the words and sentences without breaking a sweat. Their prose and logic never resembles a funhouse of mirrors, leaving the reader with no clear path forward and no predictable exit. Just imagine if a lawyer called the same action described above in bad legal writing:

> The Knicks have advanced expeditiously to the forefront position by a very formidable advantage of 11-nil.
>
> Jalon Brunson smartly acquires the basketball (hereinafter, "Ball") at the very top or apex of the key. There is an accumulation of individuals under the basketball cylinder.
>
> Brunson hurriedly makes an examination in both directions and then deliberately changes his direction, making a progression toward the cylinder to emphatically insert a closely positioned goal. Consequently, the heretofore advantage in score has *ipso facto* increased to 13-nil.

If sports fans were forced to listen to this mumbo jumbo, ratings would plummet and advertising would disappear.

To craft clear narratives and arguments, apply the spare approach to persuasive writing. It may feel awkward at first, but stick with it and clarity will improve. Make it lean—no wasted ink. Recount the facts as if chronicling them for the radio listener:

Brian Rubenstein robbed a bank in Jersey City and led police on a high-speed car chase, which lasted an hour and covered 92 miles.

Rubenstein has been charged with 17 counts of aggravated assault, four counts of robbery and one count of securities fraud.

The power of clear statement is
the great power of the bar.

—DANIEL WEBSTER[21]

B. What Is Concrete Writing?

Writers who anchor their prose in the real world are more persuasive. Science has shown time and again that concrete words are deciphered, understood and recalled better and faster than abstract words.[22]

When presented in concrete words and concrete grammar, an argument is accessible, easily consumed and processed.[23] For that reason, persuasive writers prefer plain words over ornate words, concrete images over abstract theories, precise words over fuzzy words and concision over volume.

Given the cognitive toll exacted on the reader who must slog through abstraction after abstraction, the persuasive writer reshapes and reframes abstract points in concrete words and images to jumpstart the reader's mind. As discussed in a later chapter, the key here is to present abstract thoughts and ideas in words and pictures that resonate with *at least one human sense.*

Persuasive writers want the reader to catch their drift without increasing the cognitive load, so they avoid long words, rote terminology and jargon. They infuse their work with concrete comparisons and concrete data, giving the reader a framed portrait of the point.

This chapter explores the virtue of clear and concrete writing, but first let's discuss why it's scarce.

§ 2 Reasons for Unclear and Abstract Writing

> *The minute you read something and you can't understand it, you can be sure it was written by a lawyer.*
>
> —Will Rogers[24]

I've labored and lumbered through a deluge of confusing and impregnable prose, first as a law student, then as an attorney and now as an appellate court judge. From that arduous experience, I've spotted 12 overlapping reasons for unclear writing:

(1) Law schools. Many law schools have not taught the virtue of plain and simple prose, and instead preach the vice of stylistic caution. Students are taught to play it safe; encouraged to mitigate risk. And then, when finals roll around, law students are often expected to consume, store and vomit large amounts of information on demand—without regard to lexicon or organization. That's first-rate training for drug mules or competitive eaters, but poor training for our next generation of persuasive writers.

So what should law schools do? Judge Posner proposed an alternative path. When asked how law schools could improve the quality of legal writing, he answered: "If I were teaching first-year students in their mandatory writing course, I would show them examples of good judicial writers such as Holmes, Learned Hand, and Robert Jackson. I would want them to read their work, and then try to write an opinion that would have the clarity and specificity of these famous judges. I do not know what more can be done."[25] We should heed that advice.

(2) Half-baked synapse. Clear writing only happens with time and effort. At the start, your thoughts are like a blob of clay; only with time and attention do the finer points emerge. Clear thinking begets clear writing; unformed thought yields scattered prose. Clear writers spend more time at the start to get the point themselves.

> *The writer either has a meaning and cannot express it, or he inadvertently says something else, or he is almost indifferent as to whether his words mean anything or not.*
>
> —George Orwell[26]

(3) Half-baked prose. Unclear writing is written but not rewritten. First drafts are normally fuzzy. Rewriting is an essential step in the writing process. Clarity of thought and expression are refined and improved over time. Revisit your work and make it clearer.

> *The first draft of anything is shit.*
>
> —Ernest Hemingway[27]

(4) Aversion to exclusion. Some writers are cursed with an unproductive attachment to unnecessary words and arguments. These writers cannot separate the meaningful facts and law from the meaningless static. And readers pay the price because they must read and process puddles of gratuitous ink—punctuation, words, sentences, paragraphs, headings. Readers are left to wonder what matters.

(5) Curse of jargon. Other writers are cursed with antiquated and arcane knowledge and they insist on sharing it. Buzzwords infest their routine vocabulary. Cursed writers have forgotten how normal people talk and write; they no longer feel the joy of short and simple words. Having spent their professional life in an echo chamber, cursed writers grow accustomed to shorthand and lingo, and they cannot remember how it felt before the jinx was cast.

(6) Bad arguments. Some writers have bad argument, so they sow confusion, sparking a dumpster fire and demanding your full and undivided attention. They want to be unclear. They dart into the smoke when necessary to hide bad facts or bad law. They are skilled at using vocabulary and grammar to conceal, not communicate. Clear writing is not their friend.

> *The price of clarity, of course, is that the clearer the document the more obvious its substantive deficiencies. For the lazy or dull, this price may be too high.*
>
> —REED DICKERSON[28]

(7) Authority. Unclear writing also happens when writers want to create a performative sense of formality. Researchers at MIT call this "The Magic Spell."[29] They examined why contracts and legislation are often incomprehensible and found that legal writers deliberately imbue legal documents with an abstract lofty tone to signal authority.

(8) Cycle of mediocrity. Next is the cycle of mediocrity. Each generation of advocates and judges trains the next generation to adopt their bad habits. And so it goes.

(9) Never reading for fun. Opaque writers are less likely to read outside the profession. Having never read books written for normal people, these writers are less able to distinguish good writing from bad and never truly understand what clear writing looks like. They never learn the tools of accomplished writers, or how to improve clarity with alternative word and grammar choices. This is covered in Chapter 8, Be a Reader and Writer.

(10) Fear. Scared writers avoid plain and simple words for fear of looking plain and simple, uneducated or unsophisticated. This group is concerned less with communication than their own survival.

Scared writers are plagued by the same nightmare—looking dumb to the reader. To avoid that fate, they release unintelligible words, grammar and arguments to manufacture an illusion of deep reasoning. This group is more interested in looking smart than being persuasive.

> *Some writers plump up their prose, hoping that complicated sentences indicate deep thought. . . . And when we want to hide the fact that we don't know what we're talking about, we typically throw up a tangle of abstract words in long, complex sentences.*
>
> —Joseph Williams[30]

(11) New areas. A writer is hard to understand when he is writing about things he does not really understand. Even the most accomplished writers struggle with clarity when thrown into new and unfamiliar fields. This quirk vanishes over time. As you work and gain experience, your writing improves.

(12) Long breaks. Writers often struggle with clarity after an extended break. Aristotle recognized this cause of unclear writing when he asked: "Is it because the tongue is cold that it is unable to express itself clearly?"[31]

§ 3 Fallout of Fuzzy Writing

Like a tornado or hurricane, unclear writing destroys everything in its path. When a document is hard to read, it's harder to understand and hardest to remember. Unclear writing countermands access to justice, wastes time and money and undermines the search for truth. It spawns lawsuits and longer negotiations. It also weakens the attorney–client relationship.

Access to justice. Access to justice is compromised by unclear writing for writers and readers alike. Justice is less accessible to writers who cannot marshal and present the meaningful facts and law in plain English, and who cannot explain why they deserve justice. Justice is also less accessible to readers who cannot decipher and understand their rights and duties because the legal writing is unclear, whether statutes, contracts or decisional law. This has constitutional consequences because the U.S. Constitution is brimming with abstract ideas.

Only decades after our founding, President Thomas Jefferson lamented the state of legal writing in British statutes, which he described as "incomprehensible" to all, including the "lawyers themselves." Jefferson singled out the Queen's laws for "their verbosity, their endless tautologies, their involutions of case within case, and parenthesis within parenthesis, and their multiplied efforts at certainty by saids and aforesaids, by ors and by ands."[32] He knew it was important for the people to comprehend what was legal and illegal.

> *The language of law must*
> *not be foreign to the ears*
> *of those who are to obey it.*
>
> —JUDGE LEARNED HAND[33]

Time and money. A decade ago, GE Aviation combined three units into one group, the Digital Solutions group. That group's legal department inherited seven different contracts spanning more than 600 pages. The group's general counsel, Shawn Burton, described the contracts as "clunky" and "loaded with legalese, redundancies, archaic words and wordy attempts to cover every imaginable legal risk."[34]

Unimpressed, Burton directed his staff to translate all seven contracts into plain English. With lots of hard work, seven contracts were reduced to one contract; several hundred pages were condensed to five pages.

Take this example of Burton's handywork. He inherited a 417-word compliance-with-laws clause that was comprised of five distinct subsections; even giving a shoutout to "The President of the United States." With time and hard work, Burton's team reduced that clause to 13 words:

> During the contract term, we will comply with all of our legal obligations.

The immediate reaction was bad. Burton's colleagues rolled their eyes, howling that he "missed a ton of stuff." He expected that response, however, because "it was just so jarring and different." After the initial shock, each protester relented, conceding that "everything was there."[35]

> *My utopia is two non-lawyers sitting over lunch and reading the document, understanding it and signing it.*
>
> —Shawn Burton[36]

And leaner documents caused good things to happen. Shorter contracts meant faster negotiations. GE's attorneys discovered that plain English saved them time on the front end of a transaction while managing risk on the back end. The time and effort devoted to negotiations alone was reduced by 60 percent.[37]

Customers were happy. The general counsel of Qantas Airways expressed his thanks, albeit with his backhand:

> Thanks. Australian lawyers have for a long time been dealing with redundant language in U.S. legal contracts. The drive towards plain English we have seen from GE, along with companies like Airbnb, gives us great hope for the future.[38]

The truth. The truth can succumb to unclear writing. We assume the truth exists and will prevail in its battle over lies, but that assumption often hinges on the quality of written communication. Truth is a virtue that emerges with plain language and deep thought. It is harder to separate fact from fiction when presented in a fog of words. Plain language serves as a lexical lighthouse for judges and juries who must navigate that fog.

Client confidence. Clients expect their attorneys to capture and convey the strength and spirit of their cause. When not so captured or conveyed, client confidence plummets and distrust grows. Clients spend more in attorney fees because they do not understand their lawyers the first time, which generates the need for future calls, emails and meetings. Clients are unable to make intelligent decisions, too.

To make informed decisions, clients must understand their options, which is impossible when communication is unclear.

Lawyers have a professional interest to communicate effectively with their clients. To generate reasonable expectations, the client must know their chances of success and see the path forward. Clear writing builds loyalty and yields a confident client.

How does one become a clear writer? It starts with word choice and grammar.

§ 4 Mindful Word Choice

A carpenter selects his tools based on the job. He does not reach blindly into his toolbox and grab whatever is touched first. He would never wield a hammer to patch drywall or pull a screwdriver to cut tile.

Words are the tools of persuasion. Persuasive writers pick and choose the best words for an argument. They understand the power of word choice and choose their words carefully. They choose short and familiar words, vivid verbs and concrete nouns. They spurn nominalizations, distrust adverbs and disfavor adjectives.

> *The difference between the almost*
> *right word and the right word*
> *is really a large matter—'tis the*
> *difference between the lightning*
> *bug and the lightning.*
>
> —Mark Twain[39]

A. Short, Familiar and Specific Words

Greek philosophers have long known the power of short and familiar words. Greek physician Hippocrates advised that "clearness" is "the chief virtue" of language and he warned that "nothing detracts from it so much as the use of unfamiliar words."[40] Greek polymath Aristotle expressed a similar point when he recognized, "To write well, express yourself like the common people, but think like a wise man."[41]

Persuasive writers are agile with language, but choose their words carefully. They know plenty of words—hard words, long words, irregular words and abstract words; but they know that readers thirst for concrete and familiar words. They stock their lexiconic arsenal with short, simple and concrete words. They see and hear the strength and benefit of short and familiar words, which are the inventory of plain language, easily processed by the brain and pleasant to the senses. When placed together, short and simple words create pace and momentum.

Writers who reflexively grab for long, fancy and unfamiliar words are compounding the reader's cognitive chore, proliferating the sum of syllables required to read and process the point, which slows the reader down like a bug in molasses. Learn to delete words with multiple syllables when a shorter equivalent is available. As a rough goal, two-thirds of your words should have one syllable; longer words of three or more syllables should account for less than 20 percent of your words.

Many fancy and uncommon words have plain and familiar doppelgangers. Persuasive writers choose familiar verbs and nouns over their fancier substitutes:

FAMILIAR	FANCY
stop	cease
use	utilize
try	endeavor
spend	expend
part	component

Simplicity is a choice that demands courage and experience. It does not roll off the tongue. Short and simple words are not our default setting. A good thesaurus is essential.

Eric Martínez was a lawyer before he entered graduate school at MIT to study the brain and cognitive science. On MIT's website, Martinez describes his interest as "the intersection between cognitive science and the law."[42]

In 2022, Martinez teamed with two cognitive scientists to determine why legal writing is so hard to understand, which I call the dictionary definition of a thankless task. Their conclusion? Uncommon words are too common in legal writing.[43]

Professor Daniel Oppenheimer has spent much of his professional life exploring the world of reader preference—what the reader likes and dislikes. His research shows that readers prefer short words over long ones, familiar words over unfamiliar ones, and easy words over harder ones.[44] Indeed, studies have shown that writers are seen as less credible and less intelligent when they lean on long and unfamiliar words.[45] And academicians who use plain and simple words in their research articles are more frequently cited.[46]

Persuasive writers prefer concrete language because it paves the path to understanding, directing the reader's gaze to that which can be heard, seen, felt or smelt. When readers stumble on a sentence built in concrete nouns and verbs, they can immediately see its objects, actions and relationships. This is most important when writing about complex fields.

Do not forget Rule Number One. If a longer unfamiliar word is appropriate, use it. Longer words might be more suitable, precise and even concise. Just use them sparingly and don't stack them. An infrequent unfamiliar word is pleasant to the reader—a brief cognitive strain on an otherwise brisk stroll.

RULE NUMBER ONE

Never use a long word when
a short one will do.

—GEORGE ORWELL[47]

1. *Lift the Curse of Jargon*

What is love? Members of the American Sociological Association tackled that question at their 1977 Annual Meeting, which took place at the University College of Swansea in Wales. After much spirited discussion, the members agreed the word love should be defined as:

> The cognitive-affective state characterized by intrusive and obsessive fantasizing concerning reciprocity of amorant feelings by the object of the amorance.[48]

What? I'm not sure what that means, but I do know one thing, and it has nothing to do with love. The 1977 Annual Meeting of the American

Sociological Association was haunted by the curse of jargon.

The curse of jargon is a nasty spell that represses a writer's organic preference for plain and simple words. It rears its ungainly head when you shoot from the coxal bone instead of the hip; when you give a penny for someone's cognitive processes instead of one's thoughts; when you break the fibula and tibia instead of a leg; when you compare *malum aureum* to *malus domestica* instead of apples to oranges; and when it's raining felines and canines instead of cats and dogs.

A cursed writer loses her ear for the room. She does not appreciate the narrative or perspective of the reader, does not reflect on what the reader knows and must know, and cannot see or hear what the reader sees or hears. She neglects to supply readers with basic chunks of information needed to understand later chunks of information.

The curse of jargon haunts all professions and disciplines. It is the currency of specialists when dealing with colleagues—shortcuts for fusty experts and academics to flash a membership badge. For the balance of us, jargon is unreadable. Research has proven that jargon harms the cause of communication in all fields, from astrophysics to zoology.

How is the curse lifted? You don't need a witch doctor or a special amulet. Just be mindful and gain experience. A mindful writer accounts for the reader—his knowledge and expectations—and discards a parochial mindset when necessary to make the point.

Experience lifts the curse. Cognitive linguists have found an inverse relationship between experience and word complexity.[49] The experienced writer gains courage to use simpler words and readers celebrate.

Less experienced advocates avoid plain and simple words for fear of looking uneducated or unsophisticated. University of Texas Professors James Pennebaker and Thomas Lay found that "[p]eople are more likely to use big words when they are feeling the most insecure."[50]

Princeton Professor Danny Oppenheimer confirmed it. He discovered that more than 85 percent of university students purposefully use "complicated language" when crafting essays to "sound more valid or intelligent."[51] Cognitive science has shown this fear abates with experience because the writer gains confidence and courage.[52]

2. *Even Lawyers Hate Jargon*

I have heard many excuses for the importance of jargon in law. Most are mindless. Some insist that jargon and legalese are necessary for precision between writer and reader. Not so. This excuse has been disproved in study after study, most recently by cognitive scientist Eric Martínez. "Our results suggest that in many instances such jargon can be replaced with simpler alternatives that increase recall and comprehension while preserving meaning."[53] Martinez found it best to write for an intelligent and sophisticated audience of readers who lack the patience or experience for needless jargon.

Martinez found that even lawyers preferred plain language over legalese. The lawyers who participated in the study said that plain language improved their recall and comprehension, without losing any meaning. What is more, clients were more likely to sign documents written in plain language. He concluded that lawyers cling to legalese "out of habit, laziness or a respect for tradition."[54]

Many studies have shown that jargon is hard to read and remember, so discard unnecessary jargon and legalese in favor of rapidly processed plain and simple prose.[55] When prose is thick and inflexible, question whether it is necessary. Avoid jargon if you can think of an everyday English equivalent. Do not presume what your reader knows. Subdue gratuitous complexity for the sake of clarity.

RULE NUMBER ONE

And yet, jargon is often proper, nay required. Albert Einstein said so long ago: "Everything should be made as simple as possible, but no simpler."[56] Jargon remains OK when the word has no perfect substitute.

Jargon also remains appropriate when writing to specialized audiences, where it acts as shorthand for professionals. Readers of the *New England Journal of Medicine* are more likely to read about Von Willebrand disease than a blood clotting disorder. It's more precise. An appellate brief in my court properly describes the standard of review as de novo, not as from the beginning or anew.

If you can say it in plain
English, you should.

—JUSTICE RUTH B. GINSBURG[57]

Remember, you want the reader
to invest their cognitive load on
understanding your topic, not
decoding the words you use.

—ANNE JANZEN[58]

3. *Latin Is a Four-Letter Word*

Latin is beloved by many capable judges and lawyers. *The Onion* captured this toxic relationship in its 2022 amicus curiae brief to the United States Supreme Court in *Novak v. City of Parma*, where the court decided whether parody can be criminalized:

> *The Onion* knows that the federal judiciary is staffed entirely by total Latin dorks: They quote Catullus in the original Latin in chambers. They sweetly whisper "stare decisis" into their spouses' ears. They mutter "cui bono" under their breath while picking up after their neighbors' 5 dogs.[59]

Jargon in the law is frequently dressed as Latin. When crafting and recrafting your facts and arguments, remember that informal prose is more persuasive than Latin. Avoid Latin when there's a perfect English translation available—unless, of course, you practice in Vatican City, the only jurisdiction where Latin is still the official language.

Here are nine Latin words commonly used in legal writing and their English synonyms:

Not This	But This
ab initio	from the start
circa	around
non sequitur	inconsistent statement
ad infinitum	forever
inter alia	among other things
ipso facto	by the fact
ex post facto	after the fact
per annum	year, annually
per diem	daily, day

And yet, Rule Number One. Latin should be used when necessary. Many legal doctrines, interpretive canons and legal procedures have Latin names, and Latin remains proper when referencing them:

RULE NUMBER ONE

Still Good
de novo (new)
res judicata (claim preclusion)
in camera (closed to the public)
ex parte (made without notice)
amicus curiae (friend of the court)
prima facie (proof or grounds)

4. Be Specific When It Helps

Not all words are created equal. Persuasive writers get more value from their words. When choosing words, they choose specific words to make a point better and more persuasively than the general equivalent.

For example, a persuasive writer can stress that his adversary is litigious if he chooses tenth over another here:

> He filed another lawsuit.
> He filed a tenth lawsuit.

Writers who deploy selective precision are more credible because the reader knows they know their case.

B. Vivid Verbs

A verb is the engine that powers a sentence. A vivid verb injects turbocharge. Vivid verbs imbue life and energy into legal writing, pushing it forward and helping it gain momentum. They are used to seize attention and communicate strength.

What are vivid verbs? Vivid verbs arouse the human senses by capturing familiar, tangible actions that humans can see, hear and touch.

SEE 	HEAR 	TOUCH 
Sprint	Crack	Flick
Light	Rumble	Grasp
Stumble	Amplify	Slap
Plod	Echo	Pluck
Paint	Scream	Clutch
Swing	Snap	Spike

They evoke an image, sound or feeling. You can see the light or someone stumble. You can hear the crack or even the rumble. And then words like clutch and pluck resonate with touch.

Vivid verbs are most important in legal and persuasive writing because the content is dense, cerebral and abstract. A 1976 study of 200 vivid verbs discovered that readers better understood and remembered vivid verbs.[60] Why? Vivid verbs activate the sensory and motor regions of the brain, beyond just the language regions.[61]

Persuasive writers choose vivid verbs. Snake oil? You don't believe me? Consider this example from the brief of a Liberian immigrant seeking refuge in America under the Convention Against Torture. To gain asylum, the attorney who represented the immigrant needed to show the client fled Liberia in fear for his life as General Charles Taylor orchestrated a violent coup. To make that point, the advocate first wrote:

> General Taylor *issued* a formal decree that *authorized* the rebels to *eliminate* his adversaries. The rebels *implemented* the decree.

And this is fine. More than acceptable. But counsel later returned to the first draft and this sentence, and revised it with help from a thesaurus:

> General Taylor *directed* his rebel forces to *find, torture* and *murder* his rivals and enemies. The rebels did so, *sweeping* from town to town, *searching* from house to house—*leaving* chaos, murder and destruction in their wake.

Sounds better, doesn't it? The first sentence informs you that General Charles Taylor did something to someone during the Liberian Civil War. The second sentence shows you why General Taylor was later convicted of crimes against humanity.

I hear that chuckle. With the luxury of those facts, you insist, it's easy to write powerful prose. But don't be fooled. Vivid verbs can enliven any legal prose. Consider the facts of this worker's compensation appeal:

> The driver fell asleep and plowed into a guard rail along the highway. His passenger, the claimant here, was catapulted from the back seat into the cab, landing under the steering wheel.

The same is true of procedural prose. Procedural statements need not be dreary. Just describe the action in motion, not administrative parlance:

Weak:	Pete filed a Motion to Exclude the Opinion Testimony of Dan's Damages Expert Witness.
Strong:	Pete moved to exclude Dan's damages expert.

Justice Robert Jackson knew the force of vivid verbs and used them well. Jackson is revered in legal writing circles, regularly cited as the best or among the best legal writers ever. Yes, it's true he never graduated from law school, but he understood how to wield vivid verbs:

> [The advocate] will stock the arsenal of his mind with tested dialectical weapons. He will master the short Saxon word that pierces the mind like a spear and the simple figure that lights the understanding. He will never drive the judge to his dictionary. He will rejoice in the strength of the mother tongue as found in the King James version of the Bible, and in the power of the terse and flashing phrase of a Kipling or a Churchill.[62]

Something more recent? Justice Ruth Bader Ginsburg brandished her share of vivid verbs to push her prose forward:

> Readers of legal writing, on and off the bench, often work under the pressure of a relentless clock. They may lack the time to ferret out bright ideas buried in complex sentences, overlong paragraphs, or too many pages. Strong arguments can escape attention when embedded in dense or Delphic prose. Lucid, well-ordered writing can contribute immeasurably to a lawyer's success as an advocate and counselor.[63]

Who wants more fresh, vivid verbs? Here are 100 of my favorite:

amplify	fire	marshal	rush	straddle
amble	flatten	maul	scramble	stress
blitz	float	meander	scratch	strike
bust	flout	muzzle	search	stumble
catalogue	flow	oust	seize	surge
catapult	flutter	paint	shatter	sweep
cast	fly	pare	shine	tackle
charge	hatch	parrot	slam	tally
chase	heave	plow	slap	teem
chip	hurl	pluck	slug	teeter
crush	infect	pop	smother	throb
dart	insist	push	snap	thrust
dazzle	invade	raid	snatch	thwart
demolish	lament	ratchet	sparkle	tilt
detonate	launch	rattle	sprint	toss
dismantle	leap	raze	spurn	uproot
eject	linger	rebuff	spurt	wade
erupt	lob	rejoice	stir	waffle
explode	march	ricochet	stock	whirl
fashion	mark	rip	storm	whisk

Persuasive writers mix their verbs to avoid monotony, sprinkling alternative action words that convey the same point. Thus: "The statute provides this. The statute directs that. The statute commands that. The statute states that."

A word of warning. The verb world is rife with danger. Vivid verbs must not be overused. When every verb demands a reader's attention, they lose their impact. Vary the intensity of your verbs to preserve their power.

If you know how to handle the verbs,
you know how to handle the language.
Everything else is just vocabulary.

—MICHEL THOMAS[64]

Like noxious fumes, the brain does less well when exposed to fancy or fussy verbs that possess no familiar, tangible feeling.

Fancy	Plain
exhibit	show
commence	start
maintain	keep
render	make
indicate	show, say
contemplate	think
conduct	hold

Abstract verbs have penetrated our professional lexicon. Lawyers use this tired phrasing because it's the first thing that comes to mind. Abstract verbs leave us wondering who did what to whom. They are slow and dull and best used to diminish interest and attention.

Your words impacted me.
Your words touched me.

Linguists have shown that abstract verbs are harder to process than concrete verbs.[65] A string of these words will put the reader to sleep.

C. Concrete Nouns

> *Many experiments have shown that readers understand and remember material far better when it is expressed in concrete language that allows them to form visual images.*
>
> —Steven Pinker[66]

Concrete nouns are the next most fundamental piece of a persuasive sentence. What are concrete nouns? A concrete noun describes familiar, tangible things that humans can see, hear, touch, smell and taste.

See 	Hear 	Touch 	Taste 	Smell 
Wave	Music	Stove	Apple	Skunk
Mountain	Wind	Snow	Pizza	Garbage

Concrete nouns are anchored in the physical world and handcrafted for the reading brain, a third of which is devoted to vision, and most of the rest is dedicated to touch, sound, motion and space.

Most nouns are concrete nouns. We are comfortable with them because we learned them first—juice, mama, dada, doggie. They are ideal to convey cerebral and abstract ideas to an audience of generalists. You want readers to invest their limited cognitive load on your point, not your words.

Clarity is enhanced when the
writer exercises multiple senses.

—ARISTOTLE[67]

At the other end of the spectrum are abstract nouns. Abstract nouns refer to intangible and inanimate things like ideas, concepts, feelings and qualities. Readers cannot physically interact with abstract nouns, which are experienced mentally and emotionally.

Abstract Nouns			
Dissolution	Concept	Opportunity	Aggregate
Customer Service	Rationale	Expiration	System
Enhancement	Intolerance	Theory	Valuation
Indemnification	Equitable	Consequences	Predicate

Abstract nouns enlist more of the brain than concrete nouns, requiring more cognitive effort. This increased processing demand can tax working memory and slow comprehension.[68] Many writers choose unnecessary abstract nouns because they are indifferent to the cognitive tax levied on the reading brain.

The law is complicated. Adding lexical complexity to legal and persuasive writing only overloads the reader who grows increasingly frustrated because she cannot decipher the point. Persuasion is not an option.

D. Spurn Nominalizations

Nominalizations are the most common abstract nouns. A nominalization is fabricated when verbs or adjectives are remolded into nouns. These words are abstract and inflexible.[69] Many academics and bureaucrats prefer nominalizations because they diminish the force of expression, creating distance between a writer and his words by removing the agents of action.

The organization of the examination is confusing.

●——————●

The test is disorganized and confusing.

I have implemented that correction to the order.

●——————●

I fixed the order.

Nominalizations are literary shape shifters: born a verb—free to run and jump and spin around the page—yet later banished to the world of fuzzy nouns. These wooly words are known as buried verbs and zombie nouns. They plod across the screen without anyone or anything directing their motion.

Plaintiff conducted an investigation.

●——————●

Plaintiff investigated.

It constitutes a violation.

●——————●

It violated.

Persuasive writers distrust zombie nouns because they are devoid of human senses and cause readers to break a sweat. Writers reflexively unleash these demons to blur weak arguments or obscure bad facts. To the lazy writer, zombie nouns are the factory setting, chosen because they were the first word that came to mind, all unformed and fuzzy.

Zombie nouns, unlike the verbs
whose bodies they snatched, can
shamble around without subjects.

—Steven Pinker[70]

Several experiments have shown that nominalizations are read and processed slower,[71] often with less comprehension and recall.[72] These scoundrels make things more complicated.[73]

Academic and legal writing becomes thick and stuffy when bloated with nominalizations, forcing the reader to pause, process and reprocess—like streaming a movie in high resolution over a slow internet connection.

When zombie nouns descend, your writing loses its vibrance and its texture. Zombie nouns are impersonal and abstract, draining your prose of life, color and context—akin to sleep darts for the reader. A paragraph populated with nominalizations will send readers straight to bed or the next document.

Don't believe me? Consider this sentence composed by Steven Pinker about nominalizations:

> The proliferation of nominalizations in a discursive formation may be an indication of a tendency toward pomposity and abstraction.[74]

This sentence contains eight nominalizations formed from verbs and adjectives, and it never tells us who is doing what. The sentence springs to life, however, when we reanimate the zombie nouns and add a human actor:

> Writers who overload their sentences with nominalizations tend to sound pompous and abstract.[75]

Only one zombie noun is left standing—the word nominalization itself.

Even the most persuasive writers fall into this trap. In a June 2024 opinion, Justice John Roberts hoped to fend off three feisty dissents, so he stressed that each dissent distorted the majority opinion:

> The dissents repeatedly level variations of the accusation that the court has rendered the President "above the law."[76]

The point is better made and processed with a meaningful adverb and active verb:

> The dissents variously accuse the majority of elevating the President "above the law."[77]

Persuasive writers develop an eye for nominalizations by looking for the distinct tail markings shown here, and asking whether the potential nominalization can be changed to a verb.

A third method to unmask a nominalization is to determine whether the closest verb is doing anything.

> Nominalizations tend to end in:
> SION ANCE SON
> TION ENCE

> My intention is to take an examination of the law and make an evaluation.

The inactive verbs in this sentence make room for two swollen nominalizations.

Discard nominalizations and your writing will instantly be more clear, logical and concise. Your sentences will be clear because you will have built them with concrete subjects and vivid verbs, not nominalizations.

The intention of the examination of the law was an evaluation of its formation and restoration.

The test gauged how the law was formed and restored.

Your sentences will be more logical because a vivid verb demands a precise subordinating conjunction (because, although, if) to link independent clauses of the sentence:

A continuation of the guidelines will result in increased efficiency.

If we continue to follow the guidelines, we will be more efficient.

Your sentences will be more concise, too. Zombie nouns increase word count because they draw from articles (a, an, the) and prepositions (of, by, in) and require weak replacement verbs to complete the sentence. Just sprinkle a few zombies in your prose and watch the words multiply.[78]

Take this example with and without nominalizations:

> Such descriptions of the way to Zen and its stations are almost entirely lacking in Zen literature. This is partly due to the fact that the Zen adept has an insuperable objection to giving any kind of instructions for the happy life. (42)[79]

> Books on Zen do not point the way to spiritual enlightenment, partly because Zen masters have refused to share their wisdom on happiness. (23)

Use verbs and conjunctions, which make the extra words unnecessary:

> Her blood was an attraction for a great white shark.

> Her blood attracted a great white shark.

RULE NUMBER ONE

And yet, nominalizations are sometimes best. By my count, nominalizations are good for two things:

1. Cohesion and Flow

Nominalizations capture a complex and dynamic thing in one word, which helps regulate cohesion and flow.

> We decided to cancel the concert tour for safety reasons. Our decision is final.

> The company argues the statute of limitations expired years ago. That argument is unpersuasive.

When so used, a nominalization takes the form of a pronoun or definite article, empowering the writer to marshal an earlier point without tedium or confusing repetition.

This form of nominalization makes the point better and faster. When used for cohesion and flow, a nominalization reduces the number of words required to make the point, a lifesaver for advocates bumping up against court imposed word limits:

> The fact she admitted to the crime impressed me. (9)
>
> Her admission of guilt impressed me. (6)

2. *Familiar Nouns*

A handful of nominalizations have come to represent a concept or idea. These words are so imbued in our lexicon that they've permanently remolded into honest nouns:

> Few issues have us more united in America than taxation without representation. Few issues have us more divided than abortion.

These are common in academia and the professional world. They capture a complex, expansive space in a word:

perception	intelligence
precision	cognition

The brain easily processes such nominalizations based on past experience.

EXERCISES

Exercise one. Revise this sentence without nominalizations:

> Despite all the efforts of Zen experts, however, the insight afforded to us Europeans into the essence of Zen has remained exceedingly scanty; as though it resisted deeper penetration, after a few steps one's groping intuition comes up against insurmountable barriers. (41)[80]

Exercise two. Pull a first draft. Look for nominalizations. Ask why each is used. If you cannot give a reason, then revise.

Exercise three. Pull a final draft. Look for nominalizations and ask why they were used. If you cannot give a reason, then revise.

E. Distrust Adverbs

Adverbs were invented to serve other words and phrases, like Robin to Batman, literary sidekick to superhero, offering color and commentary about verbs and adjectives. They come in at least five flavors:

Adverbs of time tell the reader when something has or will happen, pointing to a date on the calendar—*today, yesterday, tomorrow*—and general time periods—*forever, soon.*	Don't worry, I'll *eventually* get to it.
Adverbs of frequency tell the reader how often something has or will happen—*constantly, frequently, rarely, always, daily, weekly, monthly, yearly.*	Nick *usually* cared when a close friend died.

Adverbs of manner tell the reader how something happened—*slowly, beautifully, loudly, wisely*. Adverbs of manner often stand next to the main verb.	She *harmlessly* fired a weapon into the air.
Adverbs of degree tell the reader that something is intense—*very, clearly, totally*.	It's *very* obvious.
Adverbs of place tell the reader where something happened (*everywhere, here, there, under, somewhere*).	It's sunny *somewhere*.

1. *Badverbs*

Adverbs are not your friend. I believe the road to hell is paved with adverbs, and I will shout it from the rooftops.

—Stephen King[81]

Adverbs do many things for writers. They are frequently used in the law to intensify and hedge. I distrust hedge and intensifier adverbs, which I call *badverbs,* because they tell the reader what to think with no support or explanation. Badverbs are not your friend. They compromise the cause of clarity and distract from the message, breeding doubt in the reader's brain and raising questions that harm, not help, your cause.

i. Intensifier Adverbs

Adverbs to intensify
Intensifier adverbs were invented to emphasize—like an exclamation point.

Absolutely Clearly Obviously

Your argument *utterly* fails.

Most intensifier adverbs are unpersuasive; indeed, readers reflexively think the opposite. When frequently used, these screamers harm a writer's veracity, competence and intelligence. They disrespect the reader, too.

> *Surely: the adverb of a man without an argument.*
>
> —Edward St. Aubyn[82]

It should come as no surprise that words like clearly and obviously do not bolster a weak argument:

> The court outrageously found the blatantly unconstitutional statute was constitutional, which was obviously wrong and clearly reversible error.

> The court held the statute was constitutional.
> It was not.

The first sentence might convey the depth of the writer's opinion, but his word choice is unattractive and unproductive. The second sentence makes his point moderately because readers are more likely to consider it thoughtfully.

Read these sentences:

> Plaintiff is completely honest.

> Plaintiff is honest.

The first sentence hopes to convey a client's absolute commitment to honesty, but the reader is left wondering why the writer changed a binary question—honest or dishonest—into a graduated scale.

Intensifier adverbs are standard fare for lazy and unconcerned writers who want to lecture and characterize, not show and explain. The worst part about intensifier adverbs is that those writers who depend on them miss the best chance to persuade.

The truck was going outrageously fast under the circumstances.

The truck was speeding at 102 miles an hour in a school zone.

Intensifier adverbs are commonly used to camouflage an unfinished product. Writers who use intensifier adverbs to hide gaps in law and logic mistake the adverb as a literary shortcut to persuasion. They offer half-baked thoughts in half-baked prose because they lack the time or ammunition to craft an argument from scratch.

Naked intensifier adverbs are used to disguise bad facts and arguments. When so used, each intensifier adverb signifies a red flag, inadvertently erected to mark a problematic issue or fact. This use of adverbs offers a peek into the writer's mind, unmasking self-perceived weaknesses. Just remember that an intensifier adverb frequently represents the last gasp of an advocate who lacks the goods to persuade.

Don't believe me? Start looking for adverbs in opposing motions and briefs, and then ask yourself whether the adverb signals a weak or close argument.

The defendant is obviously wrong.
His case law is absurdly inapposite.

These adverbs doth protest too much, projecting weakness and breeding doubt. And remember that intensifier adverbs are like a promise. When used to characterize a fact or argument, the writer pinky promises to demonstrate or establish that fact or argument.

And yet we all use them, advertently and inadvertently. Stetson law professor Lance Long studied how and when federal court appellate judges used intensifier adverbs in appellate opinions and discovered they are most often used when things are clearly less clear in their chambers. Appellate judges were most likely to insert an intensifier adverb in dissents and majority responses to dissents, when two positions conflict and things are definitionally less clear.[83]

Badverbs suck the energy from strong verbs and adjectives. Persuasive writers use vivid verbs and concrete nouns to make the reader think what was never said. Consider this example:

> After robbing a Chandler bank, Jones led police on a high-speed car chase, spanning 25 miles of highways and residential areas in Chandler, Tempe and Phoenix, while aiming his revolver at random civilians, including a nine-year-old child, and twice firing at pursuing officers. Jones ditched his car near Mill Avenue in Tempe and ran to a movie theater, where he was arrested in the ticket line.

This paragraph has zero intensifier adverbs. And yet, after reading the paragraph, the intensifier adverbs leap into the reader's mind. Jones acted outrageously, brazenly and dangerously.

> Persuasive writers distrust badverbs. Without this literary shortcut, they must work with nouns and verbs to develop their writing, manually.
>
> Meditation

RULE NUMBER ONE

Intensifier adverbs must still be used, of course, when the courts or legislature says so. And once the writer has performed the heavy lift and proven the point, he may treat himself to an intensifier adverb. Even still, the writers most entitled to use intensifier adverbs use them the least, letting their verbs and nouns do the job.

ii. Hedge Adverbs

Adverbs to hedge
Hedge adverbs were invented to concoct wiggle room and mitigate risk—like crossing your fingers behind your back.

Arguably
Apparently
Frankly

That action is *probably* legal.

Hedge adverbs are omnipresent in academia and the law, where they are used by obsessive writers who aim to mitigate risk and cover their tracks. I don't think that's a good strategy because hedge adverbs make the writer look wordy and pedantic. Confident writers are focused on making their argument or defense, loath to sacrifice clarity at the altar of compulsive accuracy. To paraphrase Led Zeppelin in *Over the Hills and Far Away*, hedge words are those words that leave the reader guessing about what the writer ought to have known.

> *On the other hand, the sentence may be so overloaded with all its possible qualifications that it will tumble down of its own weight.*
>
> —Benjamin Cardozo[84]

Many writers first embraced hedge adverbs as a bureaucratic imperative to avoid commitment and preserve elbow room. But too often they soften the commitment.

> Jones *essentially* argues it was illegal.

To a reader, this sentence breeds doubt about what Jones *actually* argues and sparks questions about why the writer hedged. Another example:

> I believe *fairly strongly* in not lying.

How persuasive is this? It was written by convicted fraudster Sam Bankman-Fried in his rambling 250-page screed to social media influencer Tiffany Fong, which he drafted while on house arrest for his bitcoin Ponzi scheme.[85] Bankman-Fried wrote these words to defend his character and veracity. Do they help or harm Bankman-Fried?

And yet, hedge adverbs are a valuable (nay indispensable) tool for any legal or professional writer because they qualify, simplify and estimate. RULE NUMBER ONE

Allegedly is a trusted device of all advocates, who might use the word to preserve a client's innocence or stress that no trial has been held. Arguably is great if something is arguable. Almost $1 million is more concrete than $999,998.

Just be careful with them. Hedge adverbs breed doubt in the reader's mind—the polar opposite of the reaction the writer desired.

2. Good Adverbs

RULE NUMBER ONE

To be clear, I only loathe intensifier and hedge adverbs. Adverbs are helpful and necessary for thoughtful writers, offering direction to the reader that clarifies or alters the meaning of the verb:

Hardly running
Slowly cooking
Impatiently waiting
Deceptively simple

F. Disfavor Adjectives

During the 1880 school year, a 12-year-old student from Dallas was given homework. His teacher directed him to craft an essay about a living person with whom he would like to change places. He chose Mark Twain (Samuel Clemens) and sent him a letter. Twain wrote back and the pair exchanged four letters about writing. It didn't hurt that Twain was smitten by the boy's teacher.

When asked for his opinion on adjectives, Twain left nothing to the imagination. He advised the boy to "kill most" adjectives:

> When you catch an adjective, kill it. No, I don't mean utterly, but kill most of them—then the rest will be valuable. They weaken when they are **close together**. They give strength when they are **wide apart.** An adjective habit, or a wordy, diffuse, flowery habit, once fastened upon a person, is as hard to get rid of as any other vice.[86]

A quarter of a century later, Twain confirmed his disdain for adjectives in a sharp rebuke of Fenimore Cooper's flowery novel *The Deerslayer*. Cooper had an adjective habit, and Twain reminded him that adjectives lose their effect when overused:

> God only exhibits his thunder and lightning at intervals, and so they always command attention. These are God's adjectives. You thunder and lightning too much; the reader ceases to get under the bed, by and by.[87]

Adjectives are like adverbs. They label and characterize rather than allow readers to reach their own conclusion about what's *huge* or *dirty*. Facts and arguments should stand on their own. Adjectives are vague. A fabulous adjective cannot rescue a weak or inaccurate noun. Most adjectives are unnecessary, tossed into sentences by writers who never investigate whether the point is already made or can be better made with nouns.

Persuasive writers prefer nouns and verbs, not adjectives and adverbs. Read this paragraph:

> The victim was home alone when the defendant, then masked, scaled the front fence with an Uzi and ordered him to lie down. The defendant then opened the front door for three masked conspirators to enter and search the house. During that search, the defendant trained his Uzi at the victim's head.

This sentence is built with concrete nouns and vivid verbs. And yet, the adjectives pop into the reader's mind as he reads the text. The reader organically reckons this robbery was scary, dangerous and shocking. Let the reader draw his own conclusion. Earn it. Facts convince the reader, not opinions.

Naked adjectives are the worst offenders, offered with no support or explanation. How persuasive is this issue statement from a recent brief?

> The question presented below is a clear issue of law with obvious statewide significance.

It is unpersuasive because it relies on adjectives to bear the load of reason.

Persuasive writers keep adjectives to a minimum, which makes their writing simpler, more concrete and easier to navigate.

The adjective is the enemy of the noun.

—VOLTAIRE

G. Word Choice Missteps

1. *When* or *Where*

Persuasive writers are careful to distinguish between when and where. When and where are frequently used to start a sentence or sentence fragment. Contrary to rumors, these words are not interchangeable. Yes, both can function as adverbs, but the likeness ends there. Where describes a location or position. When describes a time. Let's test that point.

Which usage is correct in these two sentences?

> The concert ticket fell on the floor, (where/when) it got wet.
>
> The concert started at 8:00 p.m., (where/when) the audience was told to take their seats.

The first adverb is used to describe the floor, where the ticket got wet, so where is correct. The second adverb is used to describe the hour, which is 8:00 p.m., so when is correct. Writers learn to navigate this semantic quirk with experience and mindfulness.

2. A Home for Only

The word only is pithy and powerful. With just four letters and two syllables, this adverb casts a spotlight on one thing, action or description, separating it from the rest. Too often we squander that power by misplacing the word. The word only should touch the word or phrase it modifies. When misplaced, it may alter the meaning of a sentence:

> Fidel Castro secured only a temporary restraining order against Vladimir Putin.
>
> Fidel Castro secured a temporary restraining order against only Vladimir Putin.

The first sentence casts a spotlight on the relief secured by Castro, a temporary restraining order, so the reader knows Castro did not secure a permanent injunction or judgment. The second sentence casts a spotlight on Vladimir Putin, the person bound by that restraining order, so the reader knows Castro did not get a restraining order against Nicholas Maduro or Hugo Chavez.

To be sure, the placement of only is not always critical because it might not affect the sentence's meaning. Just be mindful when it does.

3. What About However?

The word however is a conjunctive adverb of contrast, like the words *but*, *instead* and *rather*. According to linguists, this word has fallen in popularity since the 1840s.[88] I like it to emphasize contrast. By deploying however to divide an uninterrupted sentence, the writer signals a pivot and stresses the difference between sentence fragments.

Many writers use however to start their sentences. I do not. Transitions are easiest when imperceptible and seamless—when they don't look or feel like transitions. What is more, using however to start a sentence halts any cadence or momentum. I prefer to start with the word but because it has two fewer syllables, does not require a comma and performs the same task.

4. Although and While Can Mean Different Things

Many writers confuse the words while and although. Both are conjunctions, but they're not always synonymous. Although means *in spite of* and is offered to show contrast. While can mean the same thing, but it may also express that two things occurred *at the same time*. Consider this example:

> Although the victim lived, the defendant left her with physical and emotional scars.
>
> While the victim lived, the defendant left her with physical and emotional scars.

The first sentence might mean the victim survived a violent crime but doesn't live well. The second sentence might mean the defendant mentally and physically tortured the victim during the course of her life.

Summary: Although only contrasts, it does not reference time; while can contrast and or indicate simultaneous action. Account for this quirk to avoid confusion.

5. A Word About That

The word that is controversial on my court. Walking the long hall to my chambers, I've heard law clerks joke about how the word that has been banned from their chambers. Verboten, they say. Judge-made law. Although I admire this commitment to concision, the word that has its time and place as both an adverb and pronoun.

The adverb that may be imperative to communicate subtleties:

> I would not go that far.
> I would not go ~~that~~ far.

The pronoun that may be essential to bridge a mental gap:

> Transitions are words and phrases that tell the reader what's coming next.

> Transitions are words and phrases ~~that~~ tell the reader what's coming next.

The first sentence uses that to bridge the reader from *phrases* to *tell*. The second sentence coughs and stalls at *phrases*, leaving the reader dazed and confused about what just happened.

That helps to emphasize a point, too. Consider the definitive phrase of American liberty:

> We hold these truths to be self-evident, that all men are created equal, that they are endowed by their Creator with certain unalienable Rights, that among these are Life, Liberty and the pursuit of Happiness, that to secure these rights, Governments are instituted among Men, deriving their just powers from the consent of the governed.

But many writers throw the word that after each verb. I'm not a fan. Like all unnecessary words, persuasive writers delete this word when it serves no purpose:

> Smith argues ~~that~~ the agency gave him no notice of his suspension.

> Smith argues the agency gave him no notice of his suspension.

Here the word that yields no value. Like other words, this word should not appear in your sentence unless it adds value.

Ask yourself: Does the word that add meaning, coherence or breathing room? Follow your ear. Less is more, so delete that when you can.

> Avoid using the word that too often. When in doubt, let the ear govern.
>
> Meditation

6. Beware of Absolutes

Absolutes are adverbs and adjectives that leave no room for error. They erect maximum expectations and expose a propensity for exaggeration. For purposes of persuasion, they are simple to dismantle:

Nobody believes in climate change.
Anyone would say you're wrong.
He *always* lied about his finances.
It *never* snows in Arizona.

Summary: Persuasive writers are agile with language and choose their words carefully. They know plenty of words—hard words, long words, irregular words and abstract words. Still, they know that readers thirst for simple and familiar words, so they rely on plain language to show the reader. They are comfortably understood. They use vivid verbs and concrete nouns, avoid badverbs and nominalizations, and are mindful of word choice traps.

EXERCISES

Rewrite these sentences to eliminate nominalizations, account for word quirks and use plain language.

1. The contract clearly contained numerous components.
2. Louisiana law makes a distinction between general and specific guarantees.
3. He offered testimony about his residence, inter alia, after the trial commenced.
4. There are statutory prohibitions against obviously absurd unreasonable actions.

5. He made a decision to proceed ex post facto for the attainment of justice.
6. In view of the fact that the defendant never made an appearance, the court terminated the remainder of trial.
7. Johnson is desirous of making the ultimate utilization of the real property to obtain the maximum income and return from this most valuable and unique parcel of real property containing a massive sand and gravel deposit.
8. After the expiration of the time, our team scored a touchdown.
9. If the question had been raised below, the situation might have been met ipso facto by way of additional proof.
10. Plaintiff took transportation from Paris to London when he was arrested.
11. While Jones was affiliated with the Phoenix Police Department as an investigator, he was a chaplain for two months in 2025, where he conducted Sunday Mass.
12. The erroneous statements of fact in the trial court's ruling necessitates reversal of the trial court's decision.

§ 5 *Mindful Grammar*

Grammar is meaningful. A silly example has gone viral on social media:

> Grammar is the difference between knowing your shit and knowing you're shit.

Mindful grammar is a series of good choices. Persuasive writers mind their grammar. They craft each sentence and paragraph with prescience and intention. They know what their readers want and expect, and they strive to deliver.

Grammar is a piano I play by ear.

—JOAN DIDION[89]

A. Mindful Sentences

For first you write a sentence,
And then you chop it small;
Then mix the bits, and sort them out
Just as they chance to fall:
The order of the phrases makes
No difference at all.

—LEWIS CARROLL[90]

A sentence is an empty canvas that captures and conveys a unit of meaning with a main clause and subordinate clauses. It's constructed with thoughts and ideas connected by punctuation. It can be one word or stretch to infinity as words and clauses are stapled onto the main clause.

A mindful sentence is hard to write but easy to read. It has a goal and each clause gets you there. It can unwind over several lines. It moves from shorter to longer, simpler to harder; the shorter and easier clause introduces the longer and harder elements that follow. It eschews unnecessary pageantry and subordinate clauses.

Bad writers mistake sentences as storage bins for their unformed thoughts, which are tossed in without regard to organization or persuasion. This causes the reader pain as sentences become a shapeless chorus of tacked-on subordinate clauses in no particular order.

Grammarians invented the sentence to convey chunks of thought in fragments, and those fragments are often interchangeable. Ask yourself what to feature when ordering sentence fragments.

His gun aloft, the officer confronted two escaping inmates, taking them into custody.

The officer confronted two escaping inmates, his gun aloft, taking them into custody.

The officer confronted two escaping inmates, taking them into custody, his gun aloft.

Persuasive writers shape their sentence intentionally, knowing that each unit represents a free-floating thought that needs a home—a sentence fragment to call their very own. They keep related words and information together and sequentially release blocks of information for readers to understand and appreciate each point. They know the start of the sentence determines clarity; the end determines rhythm.

We know from science and personal experience that readers have common expectations and preferences when reading sentences—from how they start to how they end and everything in between. Account for those preferences and expectations to perk up your prose. Let's start at the beginning.

Prose is architecture, not interior decoration.

—Ernest Hemingway[91]

1. Begin Mindfully

Shape your sentences, deliberately. A persuasive sentence welcomes the reader like comfort food; an unpersuasive sentence discourages the reader like hard math.

The reader craves uninterrupted, twin grammatical landmarks early in each sentence (subject and verb), preferably among the first six words. If you meet this expectation, you will instantly write more clearly and create a conversational vibe.

Persuasive writers open their sentences with familiar information. They do not begin their sentences with long opening subordinate clauses, unprimed cognitive load, adverbs or meaningless static.

i. Familiar Words or Information

To create a sense of flow, persuasive writers begin their sentences with familiar words or information, and only then move to new information. Readers fancy text that reads from old to new, simple to complex. They remember the last few words of one sentence, which propels them into the next sentence. Take this example:

> COVID-19 arrived in America in the last ten days of January 2020, generating twin medical and economic emergencies. The economic emergency was abrupt. The medical emergency arrived over time.

ii. Linked Noun and Verb

Place the subject and verb near each other. Your subject should be concrete—a word that readers can see, hear, touch, taste or smell; not an abstract nominalization. Spin your subject with a vivid verb and name the action. Sentences are wordy and indistinct when the subject is not the main character and the verb is not recounting the main character's actions.

Readers are confused when too many words are smushed between the subject and verb.

> The contract between plaintiff, who works for Motorola in New York but vacations in California, and defendant, who worked for Oracle in Delaware but vacations in Arizona, is unenforceable.

A sentence gains pace when it moves from subject to action. Any interruption slows the writing down and the reader gets frustrated.

iii. Long Subordinate Clause

Do not start your sentences with long opening subordinate clauses because they make sentences harder to understand. Compare these sentences. Each makes the same point, but which is easier to understand?

When a sentence does not introduce the subject and verb in the first six or seven words, it's harder to understand.
COMPARE
A sentence is harder to understand when the subject and verb are not introduced in the first six or seven words.

When you open consecutive sentences with these beasts, the reader has trouble knowing what the text is about.

Here's the good news. Many long openings are easily converted into independent clauses. Just look for the markers. Long introductory clauses often begin with the word although. To delete these protracted introductions, just replace although with a but later in the sentence:

Although most Scottsdale firefighters during this time preferred Mayor Joy Allen's dedication to public safety, they were livid when police found huge sums of their budget in her personal bank account.

COMPARE

Scottsdale firefighters were livid when police found huge sums of taxpayer money in Mayor Joy Allen's bank account, but many still preferred her dedication to public safety.

iv. Mindful Dating

Many writers habitually start each sentence and paragraph with a full date, whether relevant or necessary, and it becomes a habit:

On March 17, 2018, this happened.
On April 5, 2018, that happened.
On June 26, 2018, that happened.
On June 28, 2018, this happened.

When sentences open with a full date, the reader sweats. It's called unprimed cognitive load and it's not persuasive. Writers who use full dates as transitions are distracting the reader from what matters, unnecessarily impeding the reader's path to comprehension. The reader either ignores the date or spends brain power to remember the exact moment that something happened as he plows forward into still more abstract material—convinced it will eventually matter that something happened on June 20—not June 19 or June 21.

That's why persuasive writers practice mindful dating, offering regular words to express the passage of time. Ask yourself how the narrative would be explained to family or friends. Better options include:

> The next day,
> A week before,
> Six minutes later,
> Just two years earlier,
> After three hours,

And even when important, the reader often need only know the month and year, which are easier to read and remember, and fit comfortably in the middle or end of a sentence:

> Cain murdered Abel in March 1982.
>
> Road Runner sent Wile E. Coyote the contract in May 2022, but Coyote proposed an amended contract in January 2023.

RULE NUMBER ONE

And yet, full dates are sometimes required, especially when a claim or defense turns on them. So if the issue is whether a lawsuit is barred under the statute of limitation, persuasive writers walk readers through the calendar. For example:

> **FACTS AND PROCEDURAL BACKGROUND**
>
> ¶2 After undergoing back surgery on October 3, 2016, Taylor suffered burns to her back and facial bruises. On October 2, 2018, Taylor sued anesthesiologists Dr. Joyce Brothers and Dr. Ruth Westheimer for her injuries, along with The Pain Specialists of Cleveland. On October 29, 2019, Taylor filed her first amended complaint naming five nurses and their employers as defendants.

As shown here, writers can still keep it fresh, slotting the full dates at both the beginning and end of the sentences to avoid drudgery.

v. Adverbs

Be wary of adverbs in the pole position. Many adverbs placed in this prime real estate add no value and harm the cause, especially hedge and intensifier adverbs.

Shockingly. Outrageously. *Obviously*.

Ward off the desire to open with hedge adverbs and intensifier adverbs because it fosters confusion and adds cognitive load from the starting gun.

vi. Mindless Static

Do not start your sentences with mindless static or verbal tics. If paid to persuade, do not launch your sentences with throat-clearing words or equivocation, which sap energy and pace. It subdues even the worthiest argument.

It is axiomatic that X.
It may be recalled that Y.

Persuasive writers know the first words of a sentence present a singular opportunity to preview a theme or feature a fact.

A hundred thousand people were killed by the atomic bomb, and these six were among the survivors.

—John Hersey[92]

The opening of this sentence from the book *Hiroshima* captures the reader's attention.

2. Mindful Middles

The middle of a sentence has many roles. It may continue the same point introduced in the opening sentence fragment, add a new point for color or contrast, and link the opening and closing fragments. Some advocates view the middle of their sentences as a dead zone, a desolate hole to hide their worst facts and law.

Persuasive writers do not let their sentences disintegrate in the middle. They never center-embed the point. A center-embedded clause is built for confusion and hard to understand. And when a clause is embedded inside another clause, it's even harder to process and remember.[93] Consider this unreadable sentence from a brief in my court:

> To allow the City of Neverland to sidestep its obligations to Arizona Electric Company under the Loss Payable Clause, which purpose is to protect AE's collateral, because Smith failed to remove the Named Driver Restriction, which Restriction is buried in the application and not specifically identified in the Loss Payable Clause as an exception, in light of the Policy, Declaration Page, and facts of this case, is to enforce an agreement that lacks mutuality.[94]

I have a headache.

Remember Eric Martínez? He studied legal writing and found it replete with center-embedded clauses. He described this inimical practice "as a potential badge of honor for those who wish to 'talk like a lawyer' and be accepted by their profession."[95] But when asked for writing advice on legal and persuasive writing, he said to "prioritize unpacking clauses into separate sentences."[96]

Consider this center-embedded clause:

> Abel was surprised that Cain, who later murdered Abel and was punished to a life of wandering in the land of Nod where he built a city and fathered a line of descendants, came to his birthday party.

That sentence is hard to read. And yet, when this clausal material is unembedded and sprinkled into three sentences, it becomes straightforward and intuitive:

> Abel was surprised that Cain came to his birthday party. After all, Cain later murdered Abel and was punished to a life of wandering in the land of Nod. There, he built a city and fathered a line of descendants.

3. *End Mindfully*

Like the punch line to a good joke, readers pay attention to the final words of a sentence. The subject and verb have come and gone, but persuasive writers save a treat for the end, like a jaw-dropper, new and hard information or a dash of emphasis.

End sentences with information that readers do not anticipate. Look for jaw-droppers that might get lost in middle of a sentence (the grammatical jungle), and place them at the end or in their own sentence. Jaw-droppers can be introduced with a dash to pause for emphasis:

> The car barreled through the parking lot and smashed into the bus stop—seven people died.

New or abstract material fits well at the end of a sentence. Persuasive writers also wait until the end of a sentence to float new or hard information. Abstractions are better understood by readers when placed at the end of a sentence.

4. Keep It Fresh

We use overlying parts of our brains to read a sentence and listen to music. So like music, sentences should unfold freshly. Train your ears. How a writer hears a sentence foreshadows how it will land with the reader.

Vary the length of your sentences. Short, long and in between. Mix and match because short and long sentences do different things. Joe Moran captured a few of the differences in his wonderful book on writing:

> Short sentences give your brain a rest; long ones give it an aerobic workout. Short sentences imply that the world is cut and dried;

> long ones restore its ragged edges. Short sentences are declarative and sure; long ones are conditional and conjectural.[97]

Together they create the cadence.

i. Short Sentences

Sentences are shrinking. Just 400 years ago, the average sentence had about 40 words.[98] Today it averages between 15 and 20 words. Yes, texting and social media have played a role, but the trajectory was in place before those inventions. Texting and X only expedited the inevitable.

Still, some legal writers view short sentences as beneath them, used by only unserious advocates who have nothing to say or cannot say it. They insist short sentences are an ineffective and counterproductive means to persuade intellectually.

I disagree.

Short sentences are a clarion call. They hold an almost cinematic quality—dramatic and pleasing—that imparts emphasis and direction. Powerful and simple to read. Short sentences are a breath of fresh air.

I'm especially fond of the two-word or three-word sentence. These hand grenades were hand-crafted to stress a point and draw contrast:

That was wrong.	It does not.
So too here.	Not so.

As a private lawyer, Chief Justice John Roberts used these four short sentences to frame arguments and amplify themes. Each resonates in the reader's mind, not only for its concision and contrast, but for its direction. Each offers plain direction to the reader, using words that fit comfortably on a bumper sticker.

But these phrases must be sandwiched between detailed, informative prose. I use this device to connect ideas or to launch in another direction.

ii. Long Sentences

Academic and professional readers are regularly mauled by long and abstract sentences, forced to navigate a corn maze of words and phrases. Long sentences are hard on the brain.

Long sentences are hard to read and remember. They test the limits of working memory. The reader may forget the subject by the time he reaches the end. On top of that, long sentences lack emphasis and focus, causing the reader to lose the thread of relationships.

My advice is to make it skimmable. Persuasive writers fashion and refashion unnecessarily long sentences to extract and present what matters in digestible parts.

I've been told that complex ideas always require complex sentences. Not true. If anything, complex ideas benefit the most from short and simple sentences. When the facts are hard and the law is complex, it's imperative not to saddle the reader with more words and longer sentences.

RULE NUMBER ONE

And yet, long sentences are fundamental to persuasive writing. They are featured to emphasize a point or stretch a thought. Many of these sentences have inessential words, but each word adds value, thoughtfully placed as a gap in substance for readers to catch up before launching into the next sentence or paragraph.

Persuasive writers design their sentences so the reader can focus on the content. To that end, one long sentence can be more concise than a string of simple sentences because each point or idea does not require its own subject and verb.

Persuasive writers know how to elegantly extend their sentences. Once the subject and verb are installed, the sentence can unfurl less hurriedly.

A long sentence begins with a simple point and then unwraps the harder points in clear and manageable bits. It builds in anticipation, not confusion. Consider the evolution of this sentence:

> *The desert is hot and dusty.*
>
> The desert is hot and dusty, *spotted with cacti and teeming with scorpions*.
>
> The desert is hot and dusty, spotted with cacti and teeming with scorpions, *each necessary for our ecological survival*.
>
> The desert is hot and dusty, spotted with cacti and teeming with scorpions, each necessary for our ecological survival, *and yet deadly if mistreated*.

In high school English we learned to extend sentences with free modifiers, resumptive modifiers and summative modifiers. Resumptive modifiers restate the verb or noun used earlier in the same sentence. Summative modifiers appear at the end of a sentence and summarize the idea of the main clause, like this example from Stephen Wilbers:

> [One] method of connecting the trailing element to the main clause is with a word that restates or sums up what has been said, *a technique I am using in the sentence you are reading now.*[99]

Free modifiers are most popular. A free modifier is a non-essential phrase or clause that adds extra, non-restrictive detail to a sentence; it is unnecessary for the sentence to be grammatically complete or logically sound, but it serves to elaborate or specify information about the main clause. Persuasive writers freely wield free modifiers to extend their sentences.

I like to extend my sentences with present-participle phrases—a comma followed by a word ending in *ing*. This technique imparts a cause and effect relationship:

> Each hostess worked near the front door, greeting the diners as they entered.

> We interpret statutes de novo, seeking to determine and achieve the legislature's intent.

> Mother did not provide sterile supplies for the feeding machine, forcing the nurse to reuse the same bags and increasing the risk of infection.

I also extend my sentences with loose additive words and phrases introduced with a comma, like along with or plus. These words empower writers to increase the square footage of their sentences and extract greater value from the main clause.

> I use short, medium and long sentences, along with short, medium and long paragraphs.

But remember three things when lengthening a sentence. First, a string of subordinate clauses increases the cognitive toll on readers, which decreases their interest and understanding. Second, longer sentences remain viable only if the writer remains in control of the engine. And third, long sentences offer the magic that make the short ones sing.

B. Mindful Paragraphs

The word paragraph comes from Greece.[100] Early writers understood it to mean ¶—a symbol then used to show a break or pause between unbroken blocks of text.[101] Today we understand the paragraph to mean a block of text constructed with one or more sentences, all connected by punctuation.

Persuasive writers build their paragraphs with purpose. Each sentence transports the reader to the next sentence, like stepping stones across a running stream, until the reader reaches a predetermined destination. Early sentences might preview or emphasize the point and lay context for later sentences.

1. Topic Sentences and Content

Persuasive writers use topic sentences to begin their paragraphs and sentences. Topic sentences preview the point, shift the focus and stress the most important material. Busy readers cherish topic sentences. Research has shown that reading speed increases when the opening sentences of a paragraph accurately preview its content.[102]

Once the topic sentence is installed, a paragraph can traverse the point, or focus in greater detail, offering anything from factual support and background to context and decisional law. Turn to Chapter 5, Be Cohesive and Coherent, for more.

2. Fresh and Sprightly

Just as a persuasive sentence is not one thing, a persuasive paragraph is not one thing. Persuasive paragraphs are fresh and sprightly. They create pace and build rhythm, guiding the reader to a fixed destination. Vary the length of paragraphs. Shorter paragraphs are easier on the brain. Steer clear of multi-page paragraphs—one paragraph that spans a full page or more—because they cause anxiety and discourage the reader from moving forward. Readers love blank space. It's welcoming. Turn to Chapter 6, Be Compelling, for more.

> *Short paragraphs put air around what you write and make it look inviting; whereas a long chunk of type can discourage a reader from even starting to read.*
>
> —William Zinsser[103]

3. Account For the Last Sentence

A study from the 1960s showed that readers better recall the last item in a word list.[104] For that reason, persuasive writers often end paragraphs with a summary sentence or an introduction to the next paragraph.

C. Fictive Grammar Rules

Mindful grammar is not perfect grammar. It discards the hard-and-fast rules of musty grammarians who insist that ancient grammar principles be preserved. Look no further than a pair of unbendable edicts learned in high school English—never end a sentence with a preposition and never split an infinitive.

At various points in my professional career, I've been criticized for ending a sentence with a preposition. I think that's mindless. There are two reasons for this rule and neither is persuasive. One, the pioneers of our language interpreted the word *preposition* to mandate that a preposition must always precede something else—after all, the word starts with pre. Second, the same pioneers wanted to align the rules of English and Latin, and it's improper to end a sentence with a preposition in Latin.

A second fictional rule is to never split an infinitive, which happens when an *adverb* is placed in a sentence between the word *to* and *a verb*. Again, mindless. This rule originates from Latin, where an infinitive *cannot* be split because infinitives are written as one word. The pioneers thus decreed it should be impossible to split an infinitive in the English language, too. But it's not:

to boldly go
to quickly look

To demand that English grammar conform to the rules of Latin is like demanding that modern motorists comply with the traffic laws of ancient Rome. Chariots anyone? And yet, it continues.

§ 6 *Distrust Abstract Words and Phrases*

A. Dual Meanings

In 1971, Led Zeppelin released *Stairway to Heaven* and reminded us about a structural defect in the English language—dual meanings—because writers should know that words and sentences sometimes have two meanings.

About 2,000 years earlier, Aristotle warned about words with dual meaning. He recognized these words as the enemy of clear writing. "Using any word with several meanings renders the statement obscure."[105]

Persuasive writers know the English language is rife with traps that spawn confusion. Take this gem:

> The defendant read the newspaper article about the murders which he enjoyed very much.

What did the defendant enjoy? The article or the murders? Big difference.

Persuasive writers also know that pronouns can wreak havoc and sow confusion:

> Mike and Joe carpooled to work, but he left early.

This is ambiguous because the word he has two possible meanings—Mike or Joe—leaving the reader puzzled and the point unclear. Why did this happen? The first sentence fragment introduced two subjects; the second fragment used a singular pronoun. Choose words that convey the intended meaning.

Persuasive writers erase any trace of ambiguity and convey their point with clarity and precision. They know about homophones (bear and bare; principle and principal), and watch for traps in legal writing (cannon and canon).

B. Trim Your Hedges

Like a rude neighbor, unclear writers let their hedges run wild. Persuasive writers trim their hedges, avoiding the temptation or reflex to overqualify their facts and arguments in the name of full disclosure.

I've shared my opinion about hedge adverbs earlier in this chapter, but hedge words come in different flavors:

Hedge Adjectives
possible, relative,
conceivable

Hedge Verbs
seem, tend,
appear, suggest

All hedge words were invented to create distance between a writer and his words. They work like bubble wrap and are often used to disguise an unformed or uncertain thought.

But hedge words sap the reader's confidence. A writer who depends on hedges to qualify everything might sleep more soundly, but his readers are left to wonder what he's saying and whether he can be trusted.

Over the years, I've heard that hedge words are imperative to soften the tone and sound analytical or detached. Maybe in academia, but not in the real world. In the real world, hedge words spawn unimportant questions in the reader's mind.

> *Voices appear clear in proportion to the precision of the articulation.*
>
> —ARISTOTLE[106]

Many writers lean on hedge words when describing the facts, preserving a margin of error. But these writers lose the best chance to persuade. Assume you need to show that a group of plaintiffs are not good guys. On your first draft, you might describe the inmates as:

> <u>The Parties</u>. Plaintiffs were sentenced for several murders in multiple courts.

But that leaves too much on the table. With the benefit of time and deliberation, you returned to the fact section and unpacked the hedge words:

> <u>The Parties</u>. Plaintiffs were sentenced for 11 total murders in seven Arizona trial courts. Their victims included six men, four women, and a four-year-old child.

Both sentences are fine, but you cannot deny the second is more persuasive.

C. Mindful Defined Terms

Academic and administrative writers revere the alphabet soup of acronyms and abbreviations. According to one study, the volume of acronyms used in published academic and scientific abstracts increased ten-fold between 1950 and 2019.[107]

This trend is echoed in legal writing, which is suboptimal because acronyms, abbreviations and initials are abstract. Like a computer algorithm to the human brain, they are hard to read, harder to process and hardest to remember.

Persuasive writers think about their defined terms. They define mindfully for pace, comprehension and persuasion. They know that readers can process and remember strong nouns much easier and faster than last names or initials. Consider the difference in these two paragraphs:

Leah White ("L.W.") and David White ("D.W.") appeal the termination of their parental rights over M.W. and P.W. L.W. argues she did not receive due process; D.W. contends he did not receive services to reunify with M.W. and P.W.
Leah White ("Mother") and David White ("Father") appeal the termination of their parental rights over their sons ("Children"). Mother argues she did not receive due process; Father contends he did not receive services to reunify with Children.

Which is easier on the reader's brain?

This approach works across the spectrum. Compare these alternative defined terms in a commercial lawsuit:

Nicky Moo ("N.M.") and Fred Moo ("F.M.") appeal the entry of final judgment in favor of Franky Dime ("F.D."), Josh Carter ("J.C.") and Acme Realty Inc. ("A.R.I."). N.M. and F.M. claim that F.D. and A.R.I. never disclosed a sinkhole on the property, and J.C. neglected to find it.
Nicky Moo and Fred Moo ("Buyers") appeal the court's entry of final judgment for Franky Dime ("Seller"), Josh Carter ("Home Inspector") and Acme Realty Inc. ("Real Estate Agents"). Buyers claim that Seller and Real Estate Agents never disclosed a sinkhole on the property, and Home Inspector neglected to find it.

The law is complex enough without ambiguous definitions, which inhibit the reader from drawing meaningful, sharp legal points and distinctions. Avoid ambiguous titles when defining terms—like appellant and appellee. Persuasive writers understand and appreciate the mischief of ambiguous anchors, which force the reader to visit and revisit the first page and earlier text.

RULE NUMBER ONE

And yet, depending on your audience and intentions, the respectful writer may hue closely to party names and formal litigation titles. For instance, a trial judge who writes for only the parties might use last names because that audience might not appreciate a stale noun. Plaintiff and defendant are still fine when summarizing case law; class representative works best in class action lawsuits. Just be mindful, defining terms both thoughtfully and purposefully.

Persuasive writers also define terms to emphasize or deemphasize facts. Consider this example from the government's motion to dismiss a federal lawsuit brought by seven death row inmates who challenged Arizona's method of execution:

> This appeal presents an Eighth Amendment method-of-execution challenge. Plaintiffs are seven inmates who sit on death row ("Inmates" or "Death Row Inmates"), awaiting their lawful and enforceable death sentences.

This writer never forgets about persuasion. She defines the group of plaintiffs in words that advance the cause, reminding the reader who filed suit.

§ 7 Distrust Abstract Grammar

The whole tendency of modern prose is away from concreteness.

—George Orwell[108]

Abstract grammar hides in the shadows. Three common forms of abstract grammar are negative words, negative sentences and passive voice.

A. Mind the Negative

A negative word or sentence may be explicit or implicit. An explicit negative uses the word not or its equivalent to oppose an idea or action. An implicit negative lacks those direct markings but may be inferred.

Explicit	Implicit
not present	absent
not daytime	nighttime
unsafe	dangerous
not many	few
not the same	different
not often	rarely
not allow	prevent
not stop	continue
untrue	false

Negative words spawn negative sentences, which are imprecise and hard to read. My advice is to change negative statements into affirmative statements. Remember that a negative sentence sees an affirmative sentence when it looks in the mirror.

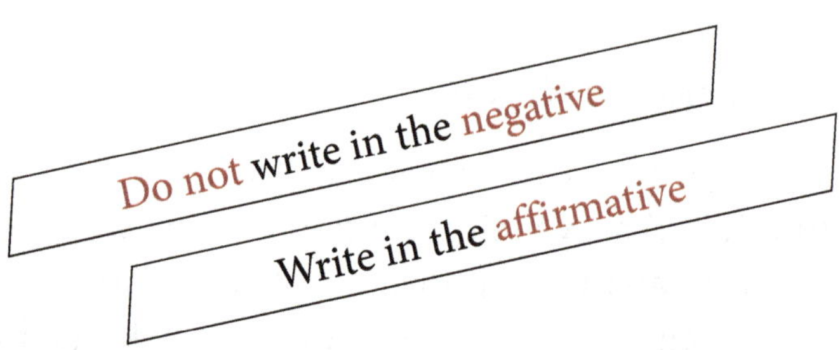

Avoid dueling negatives in one sentence. More than one negative in one sentence provokes more words and fosters confusion in the reading brain:

Before	After
Unless the pension benefits do not mature until later, they may be accessed now.	The pension benefits may be accessed when they mature.
Never imagine yourself not to be otherwise than what it might appear to others that what you were or might have been was not otherwise than what you had been or would have appeared to them to be otherwise.	Be what you would seem to be.[109]

Researchers have proven it takes the human brain longer to process a negative sentence. Why? Because readers must first understand and remember the positive to process its negation.[110] It's also dangerous. Legal writers can lose track of the negatives and inadvertently urge their adversary's point—just the opposite of what was intended.

RULE NUMBER ONE

And yet, negative words have their benefits. A writer might use double negatives to convey subtleties or forcefulness. For instance, you might want to emphasize the negative:

She was not present at the crime scene.
She was not convicted of a crime.
She was not unattractive.

B. Passive Voice

Passive voice represents the most common species of abstract grammar. Pardon the English lesson: A verb is expressed in the passive voice when its past participle is preceded by a form of was. Translated to English: Passive voice names the subject before the verb; it either ignores the agent of action or names it after the verb:

He was shot.
The investors were defrauded by the hospital.

Active voice is more transparent; it names the agent of action before the verb:

I shot him.
The hospital defrauded the investors.

Passive voice is the preset configuration for writers who think abstractly.[111] It represents semantic oxygen for politicians and large corporations—akin to the screwdriver for those who aim to deflect, disassemble and avoid blame. Passive voice is popular among writers who wish to diminish the sting of bad facts. And it's semantic oxygen for bad actors:

Mistakes were made.
Taxes have been raised.
The prisoner has been eliminated.

Consider this example, which leaves the reader wondering who decided what about which property:

> A decision was made for a valuation to be performed.

The cure? Like zombie nouns, passive voice disappears when real characters do things.

> He decided to value the home.

Passive voice has long been disfavored in legal writing circles. And for good reason. Passive voice is less clear, concise, familiar and engaging.[112] It often numbs the senses because nobody is driving the car. Active voice is more clear, concise, familiar and engaging.[113]

When passive sentences are stacked together, legal prose becomes unreadable. Take this example:

> The report was submitted after the data was analyzed. Several errors were discovered during the review process, so corrections were made. The revised document was then delivered to management.

Although this paragraph has just three sentences, it uses passive voice five times, leaving the reader confused about who did what. Turning passive voice into active voice:

> The second consultant submitted the report to the editors after the research department analyzed the data. The editors discovered several errors, made corrections and delivered the revised document to management.

Studies in cognitive science and fMRI scans have shown it takes longer for readers to read and process a point when written in passive voice compared to active voice.[114] In one study, students read the active passages seven percent faster than the passive passages.[115] Another study showed that passive voice activated regions in the reading brain associated with processing complex information.[116]

Passive voice is harder to remember. One study found that students were 25.2 percent more likely to remember information presented in active voice rather than passive voice.[117]

Why is passive voice so hard? Four reasons. First, it inverts the reader's preferred order of words. Readers expect a sentence to unfold in a particular order—subject or actor, verb or action, object or result.[118] Second, it lacks cause and effect and leaves a sentence agentless. Readers process sentences more quickly when they capture a causal relationship.[119] Third, it defies chronological order. Fourth, the human brain learns to communicate in active voice first; only later does it learn about passive voice.[120]

If passive voice is so hard for readers, why is it so common? Two reasons. First, it represents the order in which some writers think. Some writers begin with their own knowledge and work backward, writing down ideas in the sequence that something occurred to them. The net result? Writers begin with the outcome, and then throw in the cause as an afterthought. By contrast, good writers narrate a story.

Second, many judges and lawyers use passive voice as a rule to create the illusion of distance between them and their words,[121] a crime and their client.[122] One group studied when and how often the United States Supreme Court used passive voice. They reported the Court used passive voice to "cast itself as forced to act," "portray[ing] itself as a messenger, devoid of its own subjectivity and serving as a conduit through which the original intentions of the founders speak."[123] And there's some evidence this works. One study found the passive voice increased the temporal and spatial distance felt by readers.[124] But facts are facts, even when muffled in passive voice.

RULE NUMBER ONE

And yet, an unbending disdain for passive voice is short-sighted. Oftentimes passive voice is necessary, convenient and helpful. If it had no value, it would have disappeared long ago, like bloodletting and armed duels. I can think of three situations in which passive voice is helpful.

First, passive voice is helpful to link sentences and paragraphs, which nourishes cohesion. The direct object is introduced in an active (first) sentence, which is then followed by a passive (second) sentence that starts with that object. The direct object in the first sentence becomes the grammatical subject of the second passive sentence, directing the reader's attention to the act or object of the prior sentence and building flow and momentum from one sentence to the next.

Second, passive voice is imperative if an actor is unimportant.[125] For example, if you must defend the greatness of Lionel Messi when compared to Cristiano Ronaldo, which sentence is more persuasive?

> Messi has won five World Cups.
>
> The Fédération Internationale de Football Association awarded five World Cups to Messi.

Third, passive voice is priceless to focus the reader's attention on a particular thing. For instance, I used passive voice in an earlier sentence to focus the reader on the topic of passive voice:

> Passive voice has long been disfavored in legal writing circles.

Fourth, passive voice is proper if not indispensable when an actor is unknown or can be inferred.[126]

> Guns are not allowed on school property.
>
> It is so ordered.

My point is this: Sentences without characters are hard on the brain, but if the cost of active voice is unimportant words that dilute the message, then use passive voice.

> Clear prose might not be enough to push the reader forward, but unclear prose is sure to stop the reader in their tracks. Your reader is always looking for an excuse to move on.
>
> Meditation

EXERCISES

Exercise number one. Rewrite sentences to fix sentence structure. Focus on structure, not word choice or concision.

1. After returning from her honeymoon in New Orleans, the business conference in St. Lucia, and a visit to her parents in Paris, she was fired.

2. Louisiana is obliged, pursuant to the opinion and consent decree issued by the federal district court in *Cane v. Able*, 24 F.Supp.2d 209 (D. La. 2022), to expedite its development of standards.

3. Bob appealed for special action relief, reversing the entry of summary judgment on his claims for tortious interference with contractual relations and breach of the implied covenant of good faith and fair dealing, to the court of appeals.

4. After a nine-day trial, during which the superior court precluded reference to the Sedona incident, the jury found Tucker guilty of second-degree murder.

5. Police in the states of Arizona, Georgia, and Louisiana must confiscate all drug paraphernalia.

6. In the first case, which involved an oral contract for an indefinite period of time under which a distributor exclusively distributed a product though a 21-county area in which the product had not been previously sold, the court agreed it was legal.

7. His argument that defendant failed to provide a verbal warning about the spikes that caused his injury fails because he knew of the hazard and failed to conduct himself accordingly.

8. There is no time restriction for challenging a void judgment.

Exercise number two. Turn passive voice into active voice.

1. The letter was written in error.
2. It is expected that the hearing will end soon.
3. Another justice was appointed by the governor.
4. There was no discussion about the deal at the holiday party.

Exercise number three. Identify the passive voice (circle) and nominalizations (underline).

> A regard for style should ultimately be motivated by a desire for effective communication, which is essential to all human interaction. Understanding of this idea may be better instilled in students through the instruction of style in a flexible manner. This may be accomplished by presenting style as a guide to writing (perhaps applied only after a piece has been written) rather than a restriction placed upon writing.[127]

§ 8 *Abstract Things*

Make the important interesting.

—JAMES FALLOWS[128]

We have plumbed the depths of abstract words, but what about abstract ideas? Abstractions are a fact of professional life. The law is littered with them. Think of the legislative process, intellectual property and apportionment of congressional seats. These concepts or ideas are hard to understand because readers cannot see, touch, taste, hear or smell them. Readers cannot grasp or shape them in the mind's eye.

Concrete renditions of abstract material give respite to weary readers who must hurdle abstraction after abstraction like it's a track and field event. A visual image or concrete example anchors your ideas in the physical world. Research and my experience show the elixir for abstractions is analogies, pictures, charts and rhetorical figures.

A. Analogies, Metaphors and Similes

First is analogies, metaphors and similes, each a figurative device. They broadcast a high-definition picture straight to the human brain. Readers can practically see and touch your point because these devices appeal to physical senses. And again, this is particularly important in persuasive writing because the writer has room to develop the point.

Persuasive writers use analogies, metaphors and similes to revive a reader's flagging attention and increase the likelihood of comprehension. Words and images are processed on parallel pathways of the brain, and readers can better process and recall new points when presented both verbally and visually.[129]

Analogies compare two or more things to raise awareness. The point is not only to show, but to explain. Analogies represent gift baskets from mindful writers to their readers, each calculated to ease the reader's chore.

Metaphors are a species of analogy. They capture a feature in one thing by associating it to another thing. They harness our physical world and human experience to help readers understand abstract ideas, and stimulate a wave of new thoughts and associations.

Metaphors trigger different parts of the human brain. A team of researchers at Emory University found that textural metaphors like "she had a rough day" activated the same part of the brain that registers touch.[130] A member of the team described their findings as "highlight[ing] the role of neural networks, rather than a single area of the brain, in these processes." The team member reasoned that "the brain is conducting an internal simulation as a way to understand the metaphor, and that's why the regions associated with touch get involved."[131]

Aristotle was a fan of metaphors, which, he proclaimed, give writing "clearness, charm, and distinction," adding the "greatest thing by far is to have a command of metaphor," which "cannot be imparted by another" and "is the mark of genius."[132]

> *I begin already to weigh my words*
> *and sentences more than I did, and*
> *am looking about for a sentiment,*
> *an illustration or a metaphor*
> *in every corner of the room.*
>
> —Jane Austen[133]

Similes use the words *like* and *as* to compare two or more things, empowering the writer to design a vivid description. Just as a metaphor is a form of analogy, the simile is a form of metaphor. But it's different—a metaphor substitutes; a simile compares. Metaphors are more authoritative than similes and use fewer words.

All three devices rely on human experience to drive a point home. Each is used to defeat the curse of jargon and complexity, enabling the reader to instantly grasp the point. And yet, each device is unique. Let's explore each device through example. For our first example, we look to a Yiddish proverb:

ORIGINAL

What soap is for the body,
tears are for the soul.

Giving money and power to
government is like giving whiskey
and car keys to teenage boys.

Judges are like baseball umpires. Umpires
don't make the rules, they apply them.

ANALOGY

Tears are to the soul as soap is to
the body because both cleanse.

METAPHOR

Tears are soap.

SIMILE

Tears are like soap.

By comparing tears and the soul to soap and the body, this analogy makes the case for showing your emotions.

Next look to P. J. O'Rourke and his non-fiction classic, *Parliament of Whores*, about the excesses of the United States Congress:

ANALOGY

Giving money and power to government is
like giving whiskey and car keys to teenage
boys because neither can be trusted.

METAPHOR
Government is teenage boys.

SIMILE
Government is like teenage boys.

O'Rourke compares government to teenage boys, but not literally; the comparison is rhetorical.

And last, we look to Chief Justice John Roberts, who made this analogy at his confirmation hearing before the U.S. Senate Judiciary Committee:

ANALOGY
Judges are like baseball umpires because both make objective calls based on rules.

METAPHOR
Judges are baseball umpires.

SIMILE
Judges are like baseball umpires.

Persuasive writers use these devices to leverage the human experience, knowing that readers learn and understand by linking new and unfamiliar things to old and familiar things. Each device brings life and energy to persuasive writing, making difficult things easier to understand and remember. Each helps the reader to process an idea that is foreign and abstract by connecting it to something native and concrete. And each aids persuasion, although not as a direct line to reason.

How could analogies, metaphors and similes be used to persuade? By explaining amorphous legal concepts in lived experience. Let's watch each device in action, used to persuade a generalist audience in lawsuits over abstract thoughts and ideas: legislative process, intellectual property, equal apportionment of congressional seats, litigation strategy and the anticompetitive conduct of a monopolist.

Legislative process. In this lawsuit, a non-profit sued a state government over a new election statute, insisting it was hurried through the legislature "in a casual process." During motion practice, government counsel wanted the court to know the statute received no special treatment, so he reached back into his childhood for this:

> Although belittled as a "casual" process by Plaintiffs, House Bill 74 traversed the standard, well-worn path required of a bill to become a law. As many learned from Schoolhouse Rock, HB 2593 began as "just a bill" and worked its way through our equivalent of Capitol Hill—four legislative committees, majority votes in the House and Senate, and then signed by the Governor into law. Plaintiffs simply claim that standard operating procedure was not enough here.[134]

Intellectual property. In this lawsuit, Hasbro sued a small toy company for trademark infringement after learning the company produced and sold a plastic dinosaur-converting action figure. Hasbro demanded the federal district court issue a temporary restraining order for the tiny toy company to stop making the dinosaur toys, and the court scheduled a hearing. The company knew its only chance to avoid ruin was to unmask Hasbro as a bully and expose the lawsuit as specious and predatory. And so, in its response, counsel for the small toy company wrote this:

> To be sure, Hasbro has $300,000,000 in sales riding on its successful line of Transformer Dinosaur toys. But Hasbro cannot arrogate to itself a monopoly in dinosaur-converting action figures. It was, after all, the Lord, and not Hasbro, that brought the Triceratops and Brontosaurus to this earth, several hundred million years ago.[135]

Apportionment of congressional seats. Turning to judicial opinions, Chief Justice Earl Warren had to explain that federal law required congressional seats to be apportioned among the states by population, not landmass. He wanted to capture that abstract concept in plain words the reader could understand, so he wrote:

> Legislators represent people, not trees or acres. Legislators are elected by voters, not farms or cities or economic interests.[136]

Litigation strategy. In this recent opinion, Justice Elena Kagan wanted to make the point that the government changed its expert witness late in a lawsuit, so she turned to football lexicon:

> The State originally planned for Rast to testify about those matters at Smith's trial. But with three weeks to go, the State called an audible, replacing Rast with a different DPS analyst as its expert witness.[137]

Anticompetitive conduct. A final example is pulled from an antitrust complaint against 1-800-CONTACTS. Plaintiff competed against 1-800 in the contact lens market and alleged 1-800 used lawfare to suppress competition. With this metaphor, the court could see and feel 1-800's disproportionate litigation strategy:

> 1-800 unleashed the litigation equivalent of a thermonuclear war in response to the damage equivalent of a hangnail.

I have no instruction manual for crafting analogies because it's an exercise in creativity. But generally, writers should first isolate the point they want to make, and then search for an image or comparison. Think broadly about the point, not deeply. Brainstorm a bunch of comparisons and associations to your subject. Survey an online database of analogies, www.metamia.com, which covers thousands of subjects. And make sure the device fits snugly, not stretching to make the point.

* * *

A final warning: Avoid cliché. When fresh, metaphors are a form of thought; when stale, metaphors are a way to avoid thought. Take this example from Steven Pinker:

> We must give it the old college try and think outside the box in our search for the holy grail because there's no magic bullet or slam dunk.[138]

As Tracy Kidder declared: "A mind that relies on cliché does not really know what it is saying."[139] When a cliché fits, dig into the DNA for a fresh image.

B. Pictures, Charts and Tables

A persuasive writer knows the job is to move hearts and minds within the confines of ethical and evidentiary boundaries, so he integrates persuasive methods that catch the eye and steer the gaze. Writing is a visual art, so he uses all forms of persuasion, whether conventional or not.

To promote understanding of abstract concepts, persuasive writers reward their readers with concrete examples and images. When a single document, communication or picture is decisive to your case or argument, it should be placed into the text. Pictures arrest the lazy eye. A screen grab commands greater attention than unbroken text. It increases convenience, too. Busy judges are happy not to shuttle between the argument and appendix.

Take this trial brief of prosecutors in a fictional prosecution of two CEOs for price fixing. To make the point faster and better, the prosecutors plucked a damning email from the record and placed it directly in the brief:

> From: Mike Jones <mjones@monopolist.com>
> To: Peter Mills <pmills@predation.com>
> Date: Dec 12, 2026
> Re: Oral Agreement
>
> Peter: I'm not happy. We agreed that your company had Europe and we had the United States. Now I hear you just sold to a customer in Boston. Even worse, you charged less than we settled on. Call me immediately!
>
> Mike Jones
> Monopoly Inc.
> 100 SE 2nd St.
> Miami, FL 33131
> mjones@monopolist.com

Pictures are processed faster. In one experiment, participants saw pairs of items that differed in roundness (e.g., tomato, goblet) and were asked to indicate which member of the pair was more round. The objects were presented as words, pictures and word-picture pairs. The response times were slowest for word-word pairs, intermediate for the picture-word pairs and fastest for the picture-picture pairs.[140]

Visual techniques are excellent persuasive tools if not overused because they arouse the mind and eye, which fires up the visual and tactile regions of the reader's brain. Abstract concepts are more accessible and persuasive when grounded in the real world, with explanations the reader can see and touch.[141] Readers remember information better when presented both graphically and textually, likely because our brains use different systems to process visual and verbal information.

Pictures are especially helpful in property disputes, where readers have trouble seeing the dirt or buildings. This example is pulled from a decision over driveway easements:

FACTS AND PROCEDURAL BACKGROUND

¶1 Amy and Dan own individual lots in Munds Park villas, a planned community. Amy owns Lot 2. Dan owns lot 1, which is adjacent to Lot 2. Mike originally owned Lot 1, but sold it to Dan. For ease of reference, this screenshot of the recorded plat is pulled from the record:

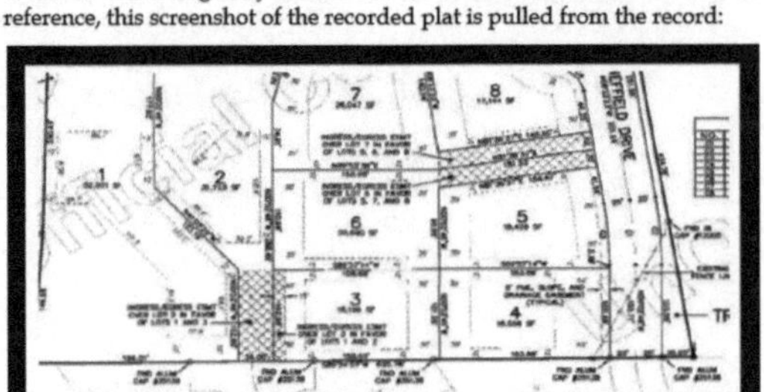

So too, pictures are useful when a party challenges a trial demonstrative on appeal.

Persuasive writers know the law is inundated with abstractions, so they strive to present abstract points in concrete terms—appealing to at least one human sense. Pictures and charts for the eye; analogies, metaphors and similes for the mind.

The soul never thinks
without an image.

—ARISTOTLE[142]

In one opinion I criticized the bar
for thinking that a word is worth a
thousand pictures. The aversion to
the visual . . . is an excellent example
of the flight from concreteness to
abstractness that is such a pronounced
feature of the legal profession's
style of thinking and writing.

—JUDGE RICHARD POSNER[143]

EXERCISES

Exercise number one. Read these quotes and identify each as a metaphor or simile.

> Writing is manual labor of the mind: a job, like laying pipe.[144]
>
> Life is like a box of chocolates.[145]
>
> Laws are like cobwebs, which may catch small flies, but let wasps and hornets break through.

Exercise number two. Pull two issues or arguments from a recent draft and create metaphors and similes for each.

§ 9 Hemingway and Orwell, Not Faulkner

To summarize our third mantra—Be Clear and Concrete—let's have some fun and watch the instructional points in action.

Ernest Hemingway and William Faulker are heralded as America's greatest writers. And yet, the men occupy distant poles on the continuum of style. Their disparate approaches paint a great contrast for persuasive writing.

These luminaries lived at the same time. Indeed, in April 1949, Faulkner listed Hemingway as one of "the five most important contemporary writers." But Faulkner delivered the compliment with invective:

> Ernest Hemingway has no courage, has never crawled out on a limb. He has never been known to use a word that might cause the reader to check with a dictionary to see if it is properly used.[146]

A reporter later caught up with Hemingway in Key West, told him about the remark and asked for a comment. Hemingway paused and leveled a lethal response:

> Poor Faulkner. Does he really think big emotions come from big words? He thinks I don't know the ten-dollar words. I know them all right. But there are older and simpler and better words, and those are the ones I use.[147]

I dig Hemingway. Do you remember reading Faulkner in high school? I do. Nightmare. His stream-of-consciousness style spawned long and hard sentences. His prose caused me to read the same sentences and paragraphs again and again. Smart guy, but reading him was a chore. Like shoveling the snow from your driveway after a blizzard.

Hemingway is the opposite. He's easy to read. Spare and direct. According to the website LitCharts.com, Hemingway used more verbs, fewer adjectives and fewer manner adverbs than other writers—a hallmark of his concise yet vivid style. The result? Decreased cognitive load. A seasoned reader can devour two or more Hemingway novels in the time it takes to navigate one Faulkner tome.

I'm convinced that Hemingway would have made a great persuasive writer. Faulkner, not so much. To make this point, let's look at their celebrated work.

Hemingway first. This is the opening paragraph of *For Whom the Bell Tolls*:

> He lay flat on the brown, pine-needled floor of the forest, his chin on his folded arms, and high overhead the wind blew in the tops of the pine trees. The mountainside sloped gently where he lay; but below it was steep and he could see the dark of the oiled road winding through the pass. There was a stream alongside the road and far down the pass he saw a mill beside the stream and the falling water of the dam, white in the summer sunlight.[148]

This paragraph employs many of the skills discussed in this chapter. Hemingway used concrete nouns (floor, forest, pine trees, chin, road, mountainside, stream), and vivid verbs (lay, blew, sloped, see). No nominalizations or gratuitous adverbs. And when used, his adverb works because it imparts more data (sloped gently). He primes the reader, gets to the main verb quickly and does not interrupt the subject-verb connection. His words are short and plain. Most words have one syllable.

Next we turn to Faulkner. This paragraph is plucked from his 1929 classic *The Sound and the Fury*:

> It was Grandfather's and when Father gave it to me he said I give you the mausoleum of all hope and desire; it's rather excruciatingly apt that you will use it to gain the reducto

> absurdum of all human experience which can fit your individual needs no better than it fitted his or his father's.[149]

This sentence is laden with abstractions. It has no topic sentence. It uses an intensifier adverb (excruciatingly), long and abstract words (mausoleum, experience, excruciatingly, individual), Latin (*reducto absurdum*) and abstract grammar (embedded clauses, single run-on sentence, pronoun confusion, no clear progression of subject to verb to object).

For one more comparison, look to George Orwell. I regard him as a master of written communication. His literary works model many of the skills presented in this chapter. Take this paragraph from *Down and Out in Paris and London*, which documents the years that Orwell spent living on the streets of Paris and London:

> You discover what it is like to be hungry. With bread and margarine in your belly, you go out and look into the shop windows. Everywhere there is food insulting you in huge, wasteful piles; whole dead pigs, baskets of hot loaves, great yellow blocks of butter, strings of sausages, mountains of potatoes, vast Gruyere cheeses like grindstones. A sniveling self-pity comes over you at the sight of so much food. You plan to grab a loaf and run, swallowing it before they catch you; and you refrain, from pure funk.[150]

Orwell uses concrete nouns (loaf, pigs, belly, bread) and vivid verbs (look, discover, grab, catch, run). He appeals to human senses. He introduces the paragraph with a preview. Orwell is firmly anchored in the physical world. He features analogies to paint a picture (mountains of potatoes, cheese like grindstones).

This paragraph is fresh. The first sentence is short (9 words), the second sentence is longer (16 words), the third sentence is the longest (33 words). He introduces new information in the context of old information.

Like Hemingway, he gets to the main verb quickly and does not interrupt the subject-verb connection. No wasted words. No meaningless or implied words. And he mindfully uses punctuation to extend his sentences. His short sentences ring like the gospel truth; the longer ones transport us on a journey.

> Although readers cannot escape the muck of law or life, the persuasive writer calibrates their prose to deliver that muck with grace and style.
>
> **Meditation**

CHAPTER 4
BE CONCISE

1 Reasons for Prolixity
2 Keep It Tight
3 Less Is More
4 Hard Work
5 Omit Needless Words

A lawyer is a person who
writes a 10,000-word document
and calls it a brief.

—Anonymous

Chief Justice John Roberts championed the virtue of concision to Bryan Garner when he explained: "I have yet to put down a brief and say, I wish that had been longer," adding "there isn't a judge alive who won't say the same thing. Almost every brief I've read could be shorter."[151]

Justice Ruth Bader Ginsburg concurred. She emphasized the virtue of concision in her chambers, directing her clerks to "get it right and keep it tight."[152]

A persuasive writer analyzes and prioritizes facts and arguments to pick and press only the most persuasive, saving what matters from the underbrush of irrelevance.

> *Try to leave out the part that*
> *readers tend to skip.*
>
> —ELMORE LEONARD[153]

prolixity

prolik•si•tee | *noun*

1. boring verbosity;
2. a tendency to speak or write at great or tedious length;
3. the state or quality of being unnecessarily or tediously wordy.

§ 1 Reasons for Prolixity

Before jumping to solutions, let's explore the problem. In an earlier chapter, we explored the reasons for unclear writing, but what drives prolixity?

Courage of exclusion. An insecure and self-indulgent writer lacks the courage to exclude and is susceptible to excess, afraid to omit this law review article or that unpublished opinion, unsure if it matters and loathe to find out. This group empties the cupboard in all documents (briefs, motions and internal memoranda), recounting an exhaustive historical narrative (useful and useless) and raising all issues (consequential or inconsequential), leaving the reader to wade through a swamp of trivial facts and trifling arguments.

A persuasive writer, by contrast, has the courage and confidence to exclude. That writer spends more time thinking about the issues and honing the arguments, which imbues the writer with greater confidence to believe they have identified the most important facts and most persuasive arguments. And this confidence is contagious; a confident writer inspires a confident reader.

> *All arts, big and small, are the elimination of waste motion in favor of the concise declaration. The artist learns what to leave out.*
>
> —Ray Bradbury[154]

You learn to resist the scenic routes with experience, drawing the straightest line and building the mental strength to exclude and delete.

Lack of trust. A lack of trust causes prolixity. When writers don't trust their readers, they laboriously recount each detail (material and immaterial; obvious and implied) as if writing for toddlers. Still worried the audience won't get it, these writers then garnish all details with adverbs and adjectives, which tell the reader what to think . . . leaving nothing to chance. Persuasive writers trust their readers because they deserve our trust.

Sophistication. Some writers think that concision is not lawyerly, which presumably means it's unsophisticated. I disagree. You display more sophistication when you take the straightest possible path and express yourself in the simplest possible terms.

Complexity. Some writers think the law is too complex for concision, and this may be true in some cases, but not often. Complexity is no excuse for verbal excess.

Cut-throat competition. Some writers are convinced our competitive society demands prolixity because the client wants every edge. They insist that no argument, no matter how trivial, may be overlooked or underplayed. As explained in the next chapter, this is wrong and short-sighted.

Prolixity on purpose. Some writers float words and arguments like a fog machine to overwhelm the opposition and hide a weakness. Sun Tzu described this tactic:

> If we do not wish to fight, we can prevent the enemy from engaging us. . . . All we need do is to throw something odd and unaccountable in his way.
>
> —Sun Tzu[155]

Learn to spot arguments and discovery requests specifically designed to sap time and energy. Do not spend meaningful time on a meaningless cause, leaving no time to absorb the record or law. Writers lose when their time and energy are misdirected at meaningless exercises.

> *Brevity is the soul of wit. Men of few words are the best men.*
>
> —William Shakespeare[156]

§ 2 *Keep It Tight*

Concision is a courtesy to your readers. A persuasive writer is thoughtful, careful to focus the readers on what matters. He describes only the important facts by asking himself what the reader must know to understand and appreciate the next sentence or paragraph. He presses only persuasive arguments. He recounts only the procedural history needed to understand and appreciate his point. He urges only the worthy arguments—leaving marginal arguments to watch from the sideline. He deletes the unnecessary noise, leaving the words that matter. And he takes the straightest path from start to finish.

My advice is to present your facts and arguments in the straightest line and in the simplest terms. Each word you write imposes dual cognitive hurdles on the reader who must *first* understand the word and *then* fit it into the sentence. An idea expressed in fewer words improves speed and pace.

Present the meaningful facts and law. To determine which facts are meaningful, ask yourself whether a fact is organically necessary and proper, or merely ornamental and emotional. If ornamental and emotional, ask yourself whether it weakens or obscures your narrative.

To determine what law is meaningful, ask yourself what legal elements are required to prevail. Consult local jury instructions to pinpoint what proof and facts are required to prevail on a claim or defense. Show your math; divulge all facts you contemplated when you created the argument or formed the opinion.

A persuasive writer accounts for the reader. He does not provide voluminous briefs that describe every fact and press every argument.

KEEP IT SIMPLE, STUPID—
NOT, KEEP IT STUPID SIMPLE

RULE NUMBER ONE

I'm not saying to omit relevant material. Don't mistake simplicity for simplemindedness; don't mistake simple prose for simple minds. When describing the law, watch the boundary between simplicity and oversimplification. Writers who make things seem too simple can inadvertently mislead readers.

§ 3 Less Is More

Words should be weighed, not counted.

—Yiddish Proverb

As if owners of an ink conglomerate, garrulous writers are loose with words. Unconcerned with word count, they use more words than are necessary to express their points. That's ill-advised because each word is a cognitive speed bump for the reader, compromising both pace and rhythm.

Lawsuits are not scored on word count. Words and arguments are like currency—their value depreciates when overused. Persuasive writers understand the inverse relationship between word count and success. Many judges first glance at the table of contents to determine the page length. If long, they read fast; if short, they read slower. Consider the advice of these lions:

Don't let your argument become long-winded.

—Benjamin Cardozo[157]

Experience on the bench convinces me that multiplying assignments of error will dilute and weaken a good case and will not save a bad one.

—Robert Jackson[158]

Strike for the jugular and let the rest go.

—Oliver Wendell Holmes[159]

This Treasury paper, by its very
length, defends itself against
the risk of being read.

—Sir Winston Churchill[160]

And yet, fewer words are not always best. Being spare with words does not mean being stingy with them. A preference for fewer words does not mean all sentences must be peeled to their shortest and leanest form. Economy in writing is a virtue that can be overprized.

RULE NUMBER ONE

Some sentences and arguments need elbow room. More words and sentences might be needed to tell a story with pacing and detail. More words and sentences might be essential to convey nuance. More words and sentences might be needed to benefit readers who learn by example or step-by-step instruction. More words and sentences might also generate a pleasant rhythm.

Consider the Gettysburg Address. It starts with six words seared into our nation's consciousness—*Four score and seven years ago*. President Abraham Lincoln had the chance to save two words and one syllable if he revised the start to read:

> *Eighty-seven years ago* our fathers brought forth on this continent a new nation, conceived in Liberty, and dedicated to the proposition that all men are created equal.

Not the same ring or punch.

§ 4 *Hard Work*

Voltaire once criticized *An Essay Concerning Human Understanding*, John Locke's classic, for having "four times too many words." And Locke later conceded the point, recognizing *An Essay Concerning Human Understanding* "might be reduced" and "might be contracted," but confessing "I am now too lazy, or too busy to make it shorter."[161]

Concision is hard work. It's achieved only after the writer masters the law and facts, and only after multiple drafts. It's science. Here's the equation:

Hard Work = Fewer Words

When briefs are bloated, it's often because the writer has not toiled over the best means of communication. Hard work enables the persuasive advocate to spot and amplify the critical issues and evidence. Verbal excess often exposes an advocate who lacked the time and energy to understand and appreciate the facts and law. The persuasive writer plunges into the record and masters the law, enabling him to bring order and organization to chaos and muddle.

Persuasive writers inch their way through every sentence they write—cutting here, compressing there. Hard work is indispensable to cut unnecessary repetition and delete unnecessary argument. The sweat and toil are invisible.

> Mindful advocates prune their prose of unnecessary clutter, both facts or law, leaving the straightest path.
>
> **Meditation**

§ 5 *Omit Needless Words*

William Strunk Jr. first advised writers to "omit needless words" in his book *The Elements of Style*, originally published in 1918, and George Orwell parroted that advice in his April 1946 essay *The Politics of Writing.*

But what does that mean? What are needless words? How do writers know when a word is expendable? I know of three candidates to amputate and one test to determine if you have needless words.

> *The most valuable of all talents*
> *[is] that of never using two*
> *words where one will do.*
>
> —President Thomas Jefferson[162]

A. Delete Unnecessary Words

The English language is celebrated for its rich vocabulary. In 2024, Webster's Third New International Dictionary listed 475,000 words in the English language; the revised Oxford English Dictionary identified 615,000 words. But any cause for celebration is dampened by the danger of verbosity.

Most writers use unnecessary words. Learn to spot and remove unnecessary words ~~that you don't need~~ in sentences. These frivolous words are baked into the language. Redundant words lurk around each ~~and every~~ corner in the English language. They expand the word count and distract from what matters.

Persuasive writers delete wordy prepositional phrases, a surgical procedure that requires no anesthetic and does not compromise meaning. These phrases add useless words when one word will do:

the reason for	why
at the present time	now
in the event that	if
concerning the matter	about
there is a need for	must
are in a position	can
it is possible that	may
prior to	before
decrease in the number of	fewer
increase in the number of	more

These examples are pulled from briefs and motions with my edits in blue and redline:

> He went there ~~for the purpose of~~ to see~~ing~~ his pregnant wife ~~at the time that she was pregnant~~.
>
> Our client must prevail ~~owing to the fact that~~ because Arizona law demands it.
>
> You have jurisdiction ~~pursuant to~~ under Colorado law. ~~It is imperative that~~ Our client must remain out of jail.

For your convenience, Appendix II has pages and pages of common bloated phrases and their leaner one-word alternatives.

B. Delete Redundant Words

Many writers use meaningless words. Learn to spot them. I hope ~~and desire~~ that you excise any ~~and all~~ meaningless words from your prose. Delete each ~~and every~~ word that adds no value.

Many redundant words are verbal tics:

> Productivity ~~actually~~ depends on ~~certain factors that~~ ~~basically~~ ~~involve~~ psychology more than ~~any particular~~ technology.

A second form of redundant words is the doublet. Our pioneers created this group of musty phrases for reasons that no longer matter. You see, the English language was kinda new and the pioneers feared that readers and listeners might not understand our native words, so they paired those words with exact foreign translations from languages (French or Latin) that had stood the test of time. It also seemed more learned.

Today you can use the English word alone if the sentence makes sense. Otherwise use the foreign word alone.

Most doublets words are redundant today:

NEED I REPEAT MYSELF	
any (English) **and all** (Danish)	**goods** (English) **and chattels** (French)
breaking (English) **and entering** (French)	**holy** (English) **and sacred** (French)
continue (French) **on** (English)	**hopes** (English) **and desires** (French)
due (French) **and owing** (English)	**new** (English) **and novel** (French)
each (English) **and every** (English)	**peace** (English) **and quiet** (Latin)
first (Germanic) **and foremost** (English)	**so on** (English) **and so forth** (English)

fit (English) **and proper** (French)	**split** (English) **apart** (Dutch)
free (Germanic) **gift** (English)	**true** (English) **and accurate** (Latin)
full (English) **and complete** (Latin)	

Doublets from other languages are just as important to trim:

NEED I REPEAT MYSELF	
aid (French) **and abet** (French)	**null** (French) **and void** (French)
basic (French) **and fundamental** (Latin)	**past** (French) **memories** (Latin)
cease (French) **and desist** (French)	**sole** (Latin) **and exclusive** (Latin)
completely (Latin) **finish** (French)	**save** (Latin) **and except** (Latin)
end (French) **result** (French)	**terms** (French) **and conditions** (Latin)
final (Latin) **and conclusive** (Latin)	**valid** (Latin) **and binding** (Germanic)
future (French) **plans** (French)	**various** (Latin) **and sundry** (Germanic)
heirs (French) **and assigns** (French)	

RULE NUMBER ONE

We cannot forget Rule Number One. Doublets have been incorporated into many statutes and writers should still use them when referencing the law.

Words that add no value to your message only diminish the force of the expression. Redundant words must not be allowed to loaf around under the shade tree while active words dig the ditches, doing the hard work to make the point.

C. Delete Implied Words

Some writers use implied words. Learn to spot and delete them. The rule is simple: Delete what readers can infer. Just remember that every word implies its general category. Omit the words that name that category:

During that period ~~of time~~, the membrane area became pink ~~in color~~ and shiny ~~in appearance~~.
He walked ~~a distance of~~ 12 miles.
The hole was enormous ~~in size~~.
He was absent during ~~the month of~~ June.
Her belly was round ~~in shape~~.
Come learn the basic~~-fundamental~~s.
What are your ~~future~~ plans?
He earned ~~the amount or sum of~~ $10.

D. Reduce the Adhesive Words

All sentences are built of meaningful words and adhesive words. That's all. Meaningful words are needed to capture the meaning of a sentence—the nouns, verbs, adjectives and adverbs that make the point. Adhesive words convey no meaning. And yet, they are needed to bind the meaningful words together—prepositions, conjunctions and pronouns.

A problem arises if the proportion of adhesive words is too high. Sentences that contain too many adhesive words are hard to read and understand because they dilute the meaningful words. The number of adhesive words should be commensurate to the meaningful words. Ask yourself how to express the same point with fewer adhesive words. By using fewer adhesive words, you feature the meaningful words and the point will resonate.[163]

Two examples:

> A trial by jury was requested by the defendant.

The adhesive words are marked in blue; meaningful words in red. What can be excised?

> The defendant requested a jury trial.

Second example. What can be excised?

> The ruling by the trial court was prejudicial error for the reason that it prevented cross-examination with respect to issues that were vital.

Adhesive words in blue; meaningful words in red. What can be excised?

> The trial court's ruling was prejudicial error because it prevented cross-examination on vital issues.

You get the idea.

Summary: To summarize this chapter on concision, I crafted a poem:

> Judges often think
> that lawyers spill too much ink
> on meaningless stuff
> that leaves the meaningful points rough.
>
> Concision is a courtesy
> afforded to readers
> by writers who care
> and not word-breeders.

EXERCISES

Exercise number one. Identify meaningful words and adhesive words; then rewrite to decrease word count.

1. There is no evidence to support Plaintiff's contention.

2. The motion filed by the defendant was meritless for the reason that it ignored the events prior to the accident.

Exercise number two. Rewrite sentences to omit needless words.

1. Based on prior experience, it is imperative that we secure a sufficient number of class representatives.
2. Despite the fact that he performed a search, the child was never found.
3. The contractual agreement provides that costs will be reimbursed up to a maximum of $1,000 dollars a month.
4. In the event that he makes a decision on whether to leave the corporation, management must be told.

5. There are two reasons the *Bonds* case is distinguishable.
6. The simple truth is that plaintiff dropped the ball and failed to comply with the clear and straightforward requirements of the Act.
7. I hope and desire for peace and quiet on all days, save and except for my birthday.
8. It is axiomatic that he breached the contract.
9. He walked a distance of 12 miles before the roads merged together.
10. A loud but incoherent murmur arose from the crowd that had gathered.

Exercise number three. Reduce the number of words in this paragraph without losing the point:

1. The Arizona Supreme Court adopted substantial changes to Rule 609 in the year 2012. Previously Rule 609 did not distinguish between civil and criminal cases; it applied equally to all cases. Nor did the previous version of the rule distinguish between defendants and non-defendants; it applied to all witnesses regardless of whether he or she was a party to the case. By adopting the distinctions between civil and criminal cases and between the status of a non-party, the

Supreme Court indicated that impeaching non-defendant with all the particulars of his or her prior conviction is required without any weighing of the mere probative value versus prejudice. Therefore, the particulars for which the testifying non-defendant witness had been convicted should have been admitted for the jury's consideration in assessing his credibility.

Chapter 5
BE COHESIVE AND COHERENT

1 Cohesion
2 Coherence

Persuasive writing demands more than clarity and concision. It also requires cohesion and coherence.

A cohesive draft uses words, logic and grammar to link each sentence and paragraph. A coherent draft unites the individual parts of that draft to make a larger point. A document or paragraph is incoherent when it covers a disjointed string of inconsistent and unrelated thoughts.

If confused about the distinction between these qualities, think of a puzzle. Cohesion is how the individual pieces fit together. Coherence is the final puzzle, fully assembled.

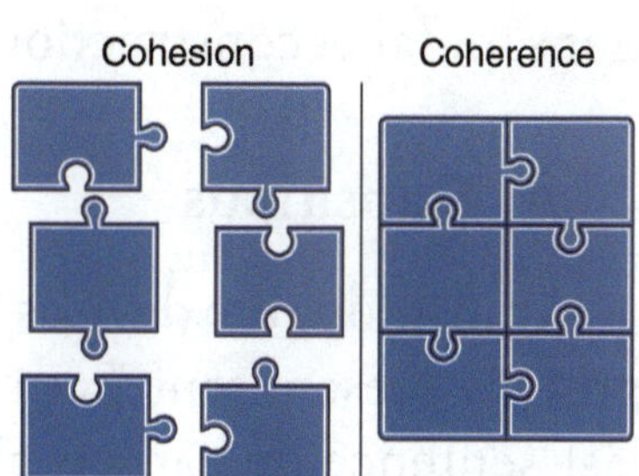

§ 1 Cohesion

Persuasive writers link their prose to create flow and build momentum, hurling the reader forward without fits and starts from one sentence and paragraph to the next.

A cohesive draft is smooth like soft jazz, leaving the reader lost in your words until the last paragraph, never tempted to check social media or text a friend. An incohesive draft is slow, like a car warranty, forcing readers to revisit earlier sentences and paragraphs to connect the thoughts. A cohesive draft is tight like rap music, bridging words and grammar to make the point. An incohesive draft reads like quantum mechanics, tempting the reader to move on rather than spend the mental energy to read and understand the point.

Persuasive writers bind their text together with assorted techniques. We discuss three here: transitions, parallel construction and pronouns.

A. Transitions

Transitions are devices that help the reader interpret the present sentence or paragraph based on the last sentence or paragraph. Transitions orient the reader to navigate the text and vary the rhythm of one's writing. Without transitions, the reader may be left to wonder how two sentences or paragraphs are related. This happens because the reading eye lingers when consecutive sentences are detached and when sentences are syntactically ambiguous.

Persuasive writers use words and phrases to bridge their sentences and paragraphs.

Words and phrases. The English language is teeming with transitions, which perform an assortment of functions, including:

- to offer an alternative (on the other hand)
- to add or supplement (further, moreover)
- to contrast (conversely, however)
- to clarify (in other words, actually)
- to concede (granted, admittedly)
- to condition (if anything, only then)
- to continue (next, afterward)
- to conclude (in closing, lastly, finally)
- to emphasize (above all, most importantly)
- to generalize (generally, ordinarily)
- to illustrate or describe (for example, for instance)
- to introduce (to start, at first glance)
- to link or compare (and, because)
- to show cause and effect (and so, as a result)
- to list a series (first, second, third)
- to order (at the outset, to begin, lastly)
- to draw a likeness (similarly, likewise, so too)
- to quantify (at least, for each, even fewer)

- to qualify (perhaps, in some respects)
- to reference (as stated above)

Shorter transitions are easier to read than long ones. Writers who habitually grab for longer transitions are increasing the burden on readers, proliferating the sum of syllables required to learn the connection. Longer transitions slow the reader down, so replace them with light and conversational transitions that create pace and momentum:

Consequently	So
Accordingly	Thus
Notwithstanding	Despite
Nevertheless	Still

Because transitions don't always spring to mind, a comprehensive list of them appears in Appendix I. I suggest you post it near your computer monitor.

The transitions I use most are single-syllable coordinating conjunctions. Persuasive writers prize the power of coordinating conjunctions to start a sentence or paragraph. These transitions are intuitive and accessible, explaining how two things are related and propelling the reader forward.

AND	BUT, YET
Unspecified link. Great for pace.	Pivot, unexpected, contrast. Contraction, caveat or other tension.
OR, NOR	**FOR, SO**
Alternative. Second negative.	Causation. Conversational. Reasoning.

ALSO, BECAUSE
Subordinating conjunctions.

Yes, it was frowned upon in elementary school, but your elementary school teacher feared the ungrammatical sentence fragment.

I have a fork. And a spoon. And a napkin.

Scholars have used coordinating conjunctions for centuries. Our Founding Fathers used a coordinating conjunction in the full faith and credit clause:

> Full Faith and Credit shall be given in each State to the public Acts, Records, and judicial Proceedings of every other State. And the Congress may by general Laws prescribe the Manner in which such Acts, Records and Proceedings shall be proved, and the Effect thereof.

See U.S. Const., Art. IV, Sec. 1.

The Holy Bible starts with 34 coordinating conjunctions (and, so) to describe what God did in the first six days. The first three are:

> In the beginning God created the heaven and the earth. And the earth was without form, and void; and darkness was upon the face of the deep. And the Spirit of God moved upon the face of the waters. And God said, Let there be light: and there was light.

See Genesis 1:1–3 (King James version).

And Abraham Lincoln dropped coordinating conjunctions in his timeless remarks drafted for Gettysburg:

> But, in a larger sense, we can not dedicate—we can not consecrate—we can not hallow—this ground. The brave men, living and dead, who struggled here, have consecrated it, far above our poor power to add or detract. . . . And that government of the people, by the people, for the people, shall not perish from the earth.

See Abraham Lincoln, The Gettysburg Address, November 19, 1863, Gettysburg, PA.

I have a simple rule. If it's good enough for the Holy Bible, the Constitution and Abe Lincoln, then it's good enough for me.

* * *

Remember that transitions can backfire. Heed three warnings: First, avoid sham cohesion. Some writers misuse transitions to create a fake connection, deploying conjunctions that represent a bridge to nowhere and nothing. They use *but* when no pivot follows, or *and* when the pivot is plain.

Second, don't overdo it. You don't need a meteorologist to know it's raining. The best signals are invisible and respect the reader—sandwich boards and bullhorns are neither necessary nor helpful.

Third, watch for quirks. For instance, the word *but* is confusing when it comes twice in the same sentence.

B. Parallel Construction

Readers revere symmetry in persuasive writing because it adds cohesion and coherence. It increases reading speed and improves reader comprehension and recall.[164] Persuasive writers weave a thread of common words and ideas through their sentences and paragraphs to reveal what a passage is about. The practice is called parallel construction and it drives the reader forward.

> The pool is in the backyard. The backyard has no fence. A fence is required for safety.

By highlighting the common words in these paragraphs, the reader understands they are reading a passage about First Amendment rights for hate speech on social media:

> The Supreme Court disagreed on one issue. That issue was whether hate speech is protected under the First Amendment. Hate speech has skyrocketed in recent years with the advent of social media. Social media companies have been unable to manage this development.
>
> Social media companies have been roundly criticized for their lack of response to hate speech. Hate speech has been allowed to run wild. Now the Court is divided on whether it's protected by the First Amendment.

As discussed in our section on passive voice, the passive construction is helpful to craft parallel structure. Active voice is used in one sentence and passive voice in the next, so the last words in one sentence are parroted early in the next. If active voice is used in all sentences, it feels disjointed.

> **Test your paragraphs.** Underline the first few words in each topic sentence, designating the subject, verb and object, and highlight words that appear more than once. You should find a discrete menu of actions and ideas.[165]

C. Pronouns

Pronouns offer an easy way to link persuasive prose. Pointing pronouns like this, that, his and hers are used to bind old and new information. When the connection is clear, it feels seamless.

> Ken Bear went shopping on March 12, 2024. At that time, he signed an amended purchase contract to acquire the goods. General Condition 10 of this contract barred Bear from returning the goods.

In this paragraph, the word that captures a full date, while this identifies a particular contract. Pronouns like his and hers are essential, too:

> Simon left the house to take a bike ride. His bike ride was exhausting but enjoyable.

But like a chainsaw and pharmaceutical ads, pronouns should come with a warning label. When used to bind two nouns, the related noun must be clear or confusion results:

> Bill and Joe left Las Vegas together with handguns, but he shot the victim.

If you represent the innocent man, this pronoun makes a difference of constitutional magnitude.

§ 2 Coherence

Persuasive writers craft their sentences and paragraphs to cohere. A paragraph, section or document is coherent when its parts (sentences, paragraphs and sections) all clarify or support the main idea.

Coherence is lost when writers randomly take side excursions to explore unrelated issues and ideas. Read this schizophrenic paragraph:

> Rats are common in the heart of Paris. Paris is expensive. France connects with Italy and Germany. I love German and American food. My friends live in America. America is the richest country in the world.

This paragraph is cohesive but incoherent because the sentences are disconnected and share no common theme. We move effortlessly from one sentence to the next, but the passage falls apart after the first sentence because the sentences have no linear sequence. The first sentence is about rats in Paris; the second is about the cost of living in Paris; the third is about countries that border France; the fourth is about food preferences; the fifth is about friends who live in America; and the final sentence is about American wealth. It's like exploring the past with someone who lacks any long-term memory.

A coherent text is thoughtfully designed and simple to navigate. Like a roadmap, it guides the reader from one thought to the next on the road to persuasion. Persuasive writers equip their readers with the knowledge required to infer and understand the upshot.[166]

Coherence hinges on organization and a logical flow of topics. Persuasive writers brandish many devices to improve coherence. We discuss four here: topic sentences, headings, priming and a thoughtful order.

A. Topic Sentences

Topic sentences have been part of the English curriculum for nearly 160 years, first appearing in a textbook from the 1866 school year.[167] And that makes sense because they're so essential to clear writing.

A topic sentence is created when the first sentence of a paragraph or section previews the point of that passage in plain and simple words. Topic sentences represent the lens through which readers consume a paragraph or section. When used, readers learn what a passage is about, know where to focus their attention, and know what to expect from later sentences as the topic sentence is unpacked.

Topic sentences wear many hats in persuasive writing. They work as newspaper headlines by previewing the main point of a paragraph or section. They work as movie trailers by seizing the reader's interest and attention. They work as road signs by linking the main point of one paragraph or section to earlier or later points. They work as the opening notes of a song by setting the tone and beat for the passage. And sometimes, they work like a snare drum roll by building excitement and expectation for a list of reasons or factors.

Two examples in red:

> Jones raises two arguments on appeal.

With that introduction, the reader learns the brief or opinion is about two arguments, and the writer can comfortably explore each argument in the next few paragraphs.

> The relationship between Cain and Abel reached a breaking point in September 2017.

With this introduction, the reader learns that Cain and Abel had a relationship and the relationship was destroyed in a particular month, and the writer can then amply explain what happened in concrete words and select detail.

For longer narratives and arguments, topic sentences become topic paragraphs. Consider this example in red:

> At issue on appeal is whether a Massachusetts court has jurisdiction to seize the assets of a California corporation. The answer is no.

With this introduction, the reader learns about the discrete issue, and the writer can delve into that issue in the paragraphs that follow. Persuasive writers use topic sentences to prime the reader and feature key words peppered in the paragraphs that follow.

Topic sentences occupy choice real estate. Research on reading patterns shows that readers, particularly when skimming, focus on the first sentence of each paragraph to determine its subject and relevance before deciding whether to read further.

In one study, researchers tracked the eye movements of readers as they consumed text electronically. They hoped to learn where the reading eye focused. What they found is important to persuasive writing. Readers are most likely to read the first sentence of a paragraph (see red) and skim the rest (yellow); they were less likely to read words located toward the end of a paragraph, on the right-hand side and further down the page (see purple).[168]

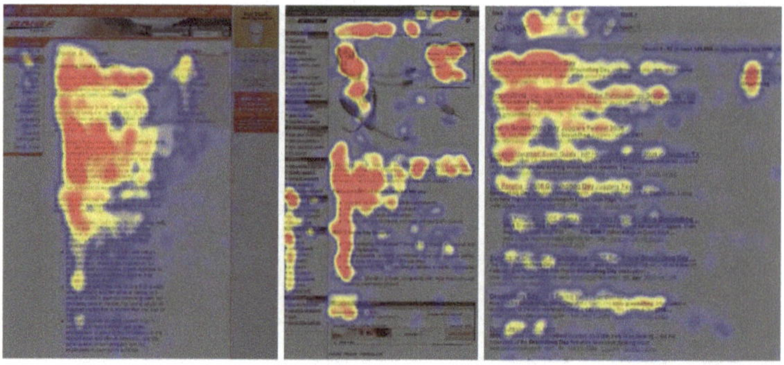

Eyetracking by Nielsen Norman Group nngroup.com NN/g

Persuasive writers start most of their paragraphs with a topic sentence because it improves comprehension, recall and reading speed. An informative, well-placed topic sentence has been shown to double recall.[169]

When the reader reads a topic sentence, it signals to his brain what's coming, enabling him to connect new and old information. This makes the topic sentence stickier because it's actively processed rather than just passing through. Topic sentences also help you organize information in your mind, making it easier to recall when needed.

Topic sentences are particularly essential for complex, abstract passages. A reader can withstand even unclear prose if he knows the destination and what to expect. When a reader does not get the point of a passage early on and moves forward without a roadmap, that passage is incoherent. Left in the dark, the reader stops reading.

Not all paragraphs require a topic sentence. You can omit a topic sentence, for instance, in a paragraph that develops an idea introduced earlier. You might also omit topic sentences when narrating a series of events.

RULE NUMBER ONE

B. Headings

For a document to be coherent, readers must see where one section ends and the next begins, which is accomplished with informative headings that announce key facts or points.

Headings are like handrails for readers. They offer general direction and move the readers forward, priming them on what's to come.[170] Psychological studies have shown that headings improve comprehension and can even influence how readers interpret the text.[171]

Headings help trial and appellate courts. Many judges first look at the table of contents to gain a general understanding of the issues and arguments in a motion or brief, and only then start to read. As a result, generic headings like "background" and "discussion" are unhelpful. They impart almost no information about the facts or arguments.

Excessive headings can annoy readers and belittle their intelligence. For that reason, I sometimes use less prominent headings to announce new content. For instance, if a particular issue turns on an eight-factor test, I might introduce each factor with an underlined word or phrase inside the paragraph, rather than give each factor its own numbered and indented heading:

> ¶1 Reasonableness. Charles Montgomery Burns characterizes the 2017 deed as "unnatural, irrational and totally out of character" for Homer Simpson. But the summary judgment record did not support that characterization. And again, naked adjectives are not evidence. *Florez*, 185 Ariz. at 526–27. This factor does not create a material question of fact.
>
> ¶2 Susceptibility. The parties presented conflicting evidence. Mr. Burns retained a medical expert who reviewed Homer's medical records and found Homer was susceptible to undue influence in 2017. Bart Simpson retained a medical expert who reviewed the same records and disagreed. This factor presents a question of fact on undue influence. *Orme Sch.*, 166 Ariz. at 309–10 (1990).
>
> ¶3 Confidential Relationship. Mr. Burns offered no evidence that Bart and Homer shared this sort of confidential or fiduciary relationship. Not even the "marital relationship" is "one of the confidential relationships giving rise to the presumption of undue influence." *Vermeersch's Est.*, 109 Ariz. at 129.

Summary: Persuasive writers use frequent headings and subheadings to thrust the reader forward from one point to the next.

C. Priming

A sentence should make the point it was formed to make and prime the reader for more. When reintroduced to words or ideas, readers enjoy cognitive ease; it makes them feel smart. A primed idea looks familiar, sounds better and feels natural. As Princeton psychologist Daniel Kahneman explained: "The experience of familiarity has a simple but powerful quality of 'pastness' that seems to indicate that it is a direct reflection of prior experience."[172]

A primed idea is also viewed more favorably because readers subconsciously process the link and trust their own judgment.[173] Scientists from the University of Michigan and Michigan State University tested this point.[174] The experiment unfolded on the front page of their school newspapers, *The Michigan Daily* and *The Michigan State News*. For several weeks, each newspaper published one of five Turkish words inside a box on the front page. The words appeared at different frequencies—from just once to 25 times. No explanation was offered for these words and those who asked for an explanation were told "the purchaser of the display wished for anonymity."

After the last Turkish words were published, the research team sent questionnaires to the entire university community, asking them to rate the Turkish words as good or bad. The results support priming. The Turkish words presented most frequently were rated more favorably than words appearing less frequently. More research has confirmed the point.[175]

D. Order

A coherent text presents the facts and law in a thoughtful order. A reader must know how everything fits together: how each segment relates to the point, how the text is ordered and the principle behind that order. A document is incoherent when questions are not answered. A first draft is frequently incoherent because writers never return to rearrange the furniture. Revisit the order after the first draft.

Readers determine whether a text is coherent. The ideal structure is simple and invisible. It resembles a straight line.

A persuasive writer orders his thoughts in the sequence most likely to inform and persuade the audience. When choosing an order, he has a bounty of options, which fall into six general categories:

Chronological	Categorical
timeline	person to person
early to late	issue to issue
old to new	thing to thing
year to year	legal issue to legal issue
present to past	case to case (decisional law)
Hierarchical	Sequential
easy to hard	the decisional path
big to small	cause and effect
degree of importance	problem to solution
degree of persuasiveness	issue to discussion
Refine/Expand	premise to conclusion
context to details	compare and contrast
general to specific	law to application
specific to general	law to exceptions
Spatial	uncontested to contested
location to location	argument to counterargument
space to space	issue to holding
state to state	

Chronological. Chronological order is most common. It recounts the order in which an event or events unfold. It works well to educate, inform and persuade.

Most writers use chronological order by default in their rough draft because it's the first thing that comes to mind. When revising for coherence, writers must revisit and rearrange that default order for maximum comprehension.

Whether chronological order is best turns on the importance of time to your theme, claims and defenses. It's great to tell a story, offer step-by-step instructions and emphasize gaps in time.

You might encounter tension, however, between chronological order and the facts, issues and arguments in your case. The narrative wants to move between points in time, but the issue or argument screams for a sequential or categorical order.

Sequential. Sequential order turns on the sequence of something—facts, issues and arguments. It joins two or more things by stressing their relationship. For instance, a discussion section might be organized by issue, argument and counterargument, or it might recount the decisional or logical path—starting with the threshold or dispositive issue and proceeding from there, or covering jurisdictional and statute of limitations issues before reaching the merits. Judges, lawyers and law students are used to processing lawsuits and deals in sequential order.

Refine/Expand. The refine/expand order organizes text from context to detail, general to specific. Writers first impart the background or framework required to appreciate the finer points. Each paragraph lights the path to the next.

Hierarchical. Hierarchical order organizes content based on its level of importance; each item is ranked above or below one another. A hierarchical order decodes which points are most significant. Arguments might be pressed from strongest to weakest. Facts might be recounted from best to worst to guarantee the most consequential are read and retained.

To persuade judges, my advice is to unveil your strongest arguments first. Judges are human. They quickly form a first impression about each case; starting with a weak argument spawns doubt.

Categorical. Categorical order allocates the facts and law into their category. It helps the reader separate one thing from another. For instance, a judge might tackle all arguments about the First Amendment before reaching the Fourth Amendment issues.

Spatial. A spatial order describes things as they appear in space. Imagine a lawsuit to quiet title to three pieces of property. The attorneys or judge might structure the facts and law by place. Psychologists say it evokes human senses and helps the reader see the facts unfold.

Take this example from a published opinion, which recounts a tragedy unfolding in different locations as a wrong-way driver plowed 30 miles in the wrong direction:

> FACTS AND PROCEDURAL BACKGROUND
>
> ¶2 Just after midnight on May 12, 2014, a motorist called 911 to report that Goliath was driving northbound in the southbound lanes of State Route 101 near Cactus Road. From there, Goliath would drive in the wrong direction for over 30 miles—spanning three Arizona freeways—before colliding with David's oncoming vehicle. Both drivers died instantly. A post-mortem exam revealed that Goliath had methamphetamine and almost three times the legal limit of alcohol in his blood.
>
> ¶3 A pair of ADOT operators watched the tragedy unfold from ADOT's Traffic Operations Center in downtown Phoenix where ADOT monitors traffic conditions and disseminates public information. The Operations Center also has programmatic control over the large digital signs mounted above and along Arizona's freeways, Dynamic Message Signs ("DMS"), which ADOT uses to inform motorists about hazards and roadway conditions in real time.

This judge started on the freeways before panning to downtown Phoenix.

* * * *

So how does one choose the best order? When unsure how to organize a document—whether an opinion, brief or motion—the persuasive writer has different techniques.

Some writers will revisit the order of their first draft and create a reverse outline, which requires the writer to distill each point—facts and law—into bullet points. Each bullet point should have no more than six words. The fact and law sections in a marital dissolution might look something like this:

Facts	Law
• Marriage • Home purchase • Improvements • Divorce and lawsuit	• Standard of review • Law of distribution • Exceptions to law • Cases that apply exceptions • Application of law

Reconfigure the original order based on the answers to several questions. Ask: (a) In what order would the reader expect to receive the facts or arguments? (b) What does the reader need to know in order to understand the next section? (c) What do you want to emphasize or deemphasize? (d) What is your theme and objective? (e) Do you want to inform or persuade? You want the order to yield a consistent and logical sequence of topics, arguments and subjects.

The second tool is called color match. A writer must read the first draft and highlight the same category of facts, issues and law with one color. Different categories are marked in different colors. This panoramic view of the text permits writers to determine which topics, arguments or persons might be out of place. If the same color appears in one document several pages apart, ask why?

The next tool requires a stack of index cards. Write each major fact, argument and topic on its own index card, then shuffle the cards and reorder them into the best order to support your position. Organize and reorganize the document to reflect that order.

The last tool to determine the best order for your discussion section is to build a ladder. Grab a blank sheet of paper. At the top, write the issue in your case with the fewest possible words (pretend you're texting a friend). At the bottom, write where you want the judge to be on the issue in the fewest possible words. Then build a descending ladder from top to bottom—each rung represents a fact, reason or argument.

* * * *

> Your job is to help the reader along:
>
> - When you choose your words.
> - When you organize those words.
>
> Meditation

EXERCISES

Exercise number one. Read the short narrative text below. Highlight the tools of cohesion with different colors.

1. We wanted to swim, but the pool was dirty with fungus growing on its walls. That was unnerving to our mother, who didn't want us to get sick. If we got sick, we'd need to miss school and that was not an option. As a result, we did not swim.

2. Moe ran the red light and plowed into the pedestrian. The pedestrian was thrown from the street onto the sidewalk. Random motorists pulled over to help the pedestrian. In contrast, Moe left the scene. Afterward, a fire truck arrived with a medic. That medic tried to revive the pedestrian, but could not.

Exercise number two. Add the transitional word or phrase wherever you think it fits best to show how one sentence relates to another. Which transitions?

1. Bob is a vegetarian, __ Todd eats meat.
2. Phoenix is sunny in the summer. _____, San Diego and Los Angeles are sunny.

Exercise number three. Draft topic sentences for these paragraphs.

1. My mother went to Louisiana State University. My father went to Louisiana Tech University. My sister went to Tulane University.
2. San Diego hits 120 degrees in August. Los Angeles hits 115 degrees in July. San Francisco has snow in June.
3. The evidence was relevant to the issue. It caused little prejudice. At the same time, it had great probative value. It was not hearsay. And the jury received a curative instruction.

Exercise number four. The sentences of this paragraph are out of order. Fix that.

1. At two months old, Child was rushed to the hospital with life-threatening brain injuries. Mother and Father are the biological parents of Child, who was born healthy in Nevada in 2011. Father was later convicted in Nevada of abusing his daughter and sentenced to prison. Child suffered severe and irreversible brain damage. She now endures many chronic and debilitating disorders, including encephalopathy, spastic quadriplegic cerebral palsy and epilepsy. She requires a wheelchair and is legally blind; cannot feed herself or communicate; and bears a perpetual high risk for seizures. Child needs full-time care to survive. This is a child dependency action.

CHAPTER 6
BE COMPELLING

1 PERSUASION
2 IMPACTFUL INTRODUCTIONS
3 A COMPELLING NARRATIVE
4 MAKE YOUR WRITING INVITING
5 MINDFUL CITATION
6 MINDFUL FOOTNOTES
7 MINDFUL BLOCK QUOTES
8 MINDFUL LISTS
9 MINDFUL PUNCTUATION
10 MINDFUL TYPOGRAPHY

§ 1 Persuasion

Greatness. Not he is great who can alter matter, but he who can alter my state of mind.

—RALPH WALDO EMERSON[176]

What makes someone read and adopt your position? Aristotle defined persuasion as a combination of ethos, pathos and logos. Ethos lives in the bond between reader and writer. Pathos lives in the heart and is moved by emotion. Logos lives in the brain and is moved by intellect.

My definition is less complicated. I define persuasion as seizing a reader's interest and attention for long enough to move his heart and mind.

To seize a reader's interest and attention, your words must prevail in an ever-competitive world for human curiosity. The number of words devoted to a point should correspond to its importance in the case. Persuasion is a straight road; no need to force readers onto the longer, scenic routes littered with unnecessary things.

To move a reader's heart and mind, you must capture and convey hard things in understandable prose. Your point is more likely to land when delivered with clarity and concision. Avoid words or issues that distract or confuse the reader. Make your point calmly and respectfully. Any passion in persuasive prose should spring from a clear and well-reasoned presentation, not intensifier adverbs or background noise.

This chapter is about mindful persuasion, which is laser focused on the audience and aims to ease the reader's path. It all starts with an impactful introduction.

§ 2 Impactful Introductions

A great introduction is fine art—crafted with great care and purpose. A first impression matters. If the reader never reads past the first paragraph, he will never read your brilliant narrative or argument. An introduction should offer context and grab the reader's interest. Persuasive writers craft introductions to arrest the lazy eye. At a minimum, that means a killer first sentence and a roadmap.

A. The First Sentence or Paragraph

An opening line should invite the reader to begin the story. It should say: Listen. Come in here. You want to know about this. How can a writer extend an appealing invitation; one that's difficult, even, to refuse?

—STEPHEN KING[177]

The first sentence or paragraph of your motion or missive is choice location—Manhattan skyline. It presents a singular chance to set the scene, strike the tone, persuade, connect and impress.

> Clarity is essential at the start. A good beginning is clear and introduces a thread that runs through your prose.
>
> Meditation

Do not spoil this singular chance to persuade with archaic formalism, reflexive legalese or snappy quotes from former presidents. You might think it's meaningful, but it's dead air to the reader who has no context to appreciate what you're saying.

Journalists prize the first sentence and paragraph, knowing that interest and attention wane over time. Do not waste this space by parroting the full procedural name of your motion or response, which should be available in the caption above. You know what I mean—cue the trumpets:

> COMES NOW the Defendant, by and through counsel undersigned, and respectfully submits this Response in Opposition to Plaintiff Old School Unlimited, L.L.C.'s ("OSU") Motion to Dismiss for Failure to State a Claim Pursuant to Rule 12(b)(6) dated February 6, 2023.

Don't bury the lede. By my count, persuasive writers have seven overlapping, non-exclusive strategies for the first sentence or paragraph. Depending on your goals, analysis and strategy, you might fashion a first sentence to:

1. Educate with context. Persuasive writers may use the first sentence or paragraphs of briefs and motions to lay a concrete foundation on which to build their case. Legal writing is a perilous journey, so hold the reader's hand.

Let's watch this strategy in action. This first example comes from the State of Arizona's motion to dismiss a local municipality's lawsuit. The municipality preemptively sued for a declaratory judgment that it need not comply with state law. In the opening sentence of its opening brief, the state offered the larger context and previewed why the city loses:

> This case concerns the hierarchy of Arizona state government.

A second example is taken from the brief of a Liberian immigrant who sought refuge in America under the Convention Against Torture. In the opening sentence of his opening brief, the immigrant offers the procedural and legal context, including the type of case and relevant laws, before turning to persuasion:

> This is an immigration case in which Petitioner John Doe sought but was denied a deferral of his removal to Liberia under the Convention Against Torture. Mr. Doe is a Liberian national who witnessed and experienced ghastly horrors and atrocities in his homeland, where he was forced to watch the beheading of his father and forced by rebels to watch his mother dance with the decapitated head to avoid the same fate herself. This is not contested.

With this first sentence, the reader learns the procedural posture, relevant laws, the immigrant's nation of origin and what the case is generally about, before turning to persuasion in the second and third sentences.

2. Frame the dispositive issue. The first sentence is a natural place to feature a dispositive issue. By starting with a short issue statement, the writer winnows the dispute to one question and primes the reader for more:

> The only issue for this Court is whether qualified immunity shields a prosecutor from personal liability for serving and executing two court-issued seizure warrants. The answer remains "yes," and the Court should enter summary judgment against Plaintiffs on the remanded claims.

This introduction must be crafted with care because opposing counsel is sure to seize upon a poorly worded or formed issue statement.

3. Simplify the complex. The first sentence is ideal to simplify what is complex. Briefs and memos can be daunting when the law is complicated and facts are opaque. For instance, assume your case turns on a 243-page collective bargaining agreement

with 40 sections, 22 subsections and 14 addenda. You might start that motion, brief or memo:

> This lawsuit is about a contract.

With this sentence, the lawsuit seems plain and approachable.

4. Explain what you want. Many writers bury their request for relief, making it hard for courts to grant them relief. The first sentence is well-positioned to identify what you want.

> David Inc. moves this Court for a temporary restraining order and preliminary injunction prohibiting Goliath Inc. from acquiring David's patent portfolio at a commercial auction set for July 28, 2018.

5. Draw the sting. The first sentence can elegantly draw the sting. This example comes from a lawsuit filed by several death row inmates who challenged the lethal injection protocol of the state department of corrections, which, the inmates insisted, abridged their Eighth Amendment rights. Most of the arguments lacked merit based on current binding precedent, but the state understood the death penalty was a sensitive, controversial issue, so this was the first sentence of its motion to dismiss:

> While capital punishment can raise hard questions, this case does not.

Persuasive writers know that concession makes them look more reasonable and builds credibility with judicial officers.

6. Introduce a persuasive theme. The first sentence is hand-crafted to engage emotion and intellect. Grab a reader from the go. This opening sentence comes from the opening brief of same-sex marriage proponents in their quest for constitutional protection:

> This case is about marriage—the most important relation in life—and equality—the most essential principle of the American dream, from the Declaration of Independence, to the Gettysburg Address, to the Fourteenth Amendment.[178]

You want the reader to read more than the first sentence, so use that spot to gain interest and persuade. This sentence comes from the brief of a television station sued by a person who wanted a seat on the debate stage for a nationally televised presidential debate. To persuade the court from the outset, the station started with:

> This case is about a serial litigant and four-time presidential candidate named John Doe who filed three lawsuits in three federal

> district courts against dozens of broadcasters who were never served with process.

With this first sentence, the reader immediately knows this was not plaintiff's first rodeo as a candidate or litigant.

A persuasive theme often requires more than one sentence or paragraph. Take this opening paragraph from a competitor's antitrust complaint against 1-800-CONTACTS:

> This lawsuit is about 1-800's bold and unlawful crusade to obtain or maintain its dominant position in the direct-to-consumer market for replacement contact lenses, and the horizontal agreements that 1-800 extracted from its direct competitors to restrict output and restrain trade. Notwithstanding its carefully crafted image, 1-800 has battled to censor and impede the universe of information that can be passed on to consumers; and conspired to ensure that consumers never taste the fruits of competition.

With this first sentence, the reader learns about an anticompetitive business model and how it harms consumers.

7. Deter interest and attention. The six alternatives described above assume the writer wants the attention. But a persuasive writer knows the best

opening in some cases is to deter interest and deflect attention, inviting a cursory affirmance. *Move along, there's nothing to see here.*

* * *

Let's watch six of these strategies in action. Still in private practice, John Roberts represented Hartford Insurance in the wake of our national tragedy on September 11, 2001. Hartford insured the World Trade Center, yet denied the insurance claims of survivors and their families, who later sued Hartford, and it reached the Second Circuit. In Hartford's answering brief, Roberts combined many of these strategies in his first sentence:

> Although the circumstances giving rise to this insurance coverage litigation are momentous, the merits of the dispute between Hartford and the Insureds present a straightforward matter of interpretation of the terms of a contract under well-settled legal principles.[179]

With this first sentence, Roberts deployed six strategies—he drew the sting, discouraged interest and attention, educated with context, introduced a persuasive theme, simplified the complex and framed the dispositive issue.

What's so hard about that first sentence is that you're stuck with it. Everything else is going to flow out of that sentence. And by the time you've laid down the first two sentences, your options are all gone.

—JOAN DIDION[180]

B. The Roadmap

With a killer first sentence in place, the persuasive writer supplies a roadmap. By roadmap, I mean an explanation of what you want and why you win in the fewest number of words. If you cannot say it in 75 words or less, you might not understand the issue and neither will your reader.

This example is from Walter Dellinger when he represented the District of Columbia before the U.S. Supreme Court in the landmark *Heller* case:

> The decision is wrong for three separate reasons, each of which independently warrants reversal and entry of judgment for the District: (1) The Nation's capital has regulated guns for two centuries. (2) Heller owns handguns and long guns but stores them outside the District. (3) A divided panel of the court of appeals reversed. *District of Columbia v. Heller*, 554 U.S. 570 (2008) (Petitioners' opening brief).

Expand the target for success. If your client wins for three different reasons, each of which is dispositive, impart that knowledge with a list. You might use underlined mini-headings with full sentence summaries; then briefly explain what your client wants.

In this example a government defendant lists three independent reasons why several non-profit plaintiffs lacked standing in federal court to challenge a criminal statute that prohibited abortions when performed to ensure the sex or race of a child:

> Plaintiffs lack standing to raise their equal protection claim for three independent and equally dispositive reasons:
>
> - **Stigma does not meet Article III injury requirement**. Plaintiffs' sole alleged injury is stigma, which is insufficient to convey constitutional standing.
> - **No genuine threat of prosecution**. Plaintiffs do not intend to engage in conduct prohibited under the challenged statutes. Nor could they. Even if Plaintiffs or their members intended to obtain a race or sex-based abortion, the statutes expressly exclude pregnant females from liability.
> - **No standing to assert generalized grievance**. Plaintiffs seek no more than to vindicate their own value preference through federal courts, which is not permitted. An intense dissatisfaction with government cannot substitute for actual injury under Article III.
>
> Defendants thus move the Court to dismiss the Complaint with prejudice for lack of subject matter jurisdiction pursuant to Rule 12(b)(1), Fed. R. Civ. P.

As an added benefit, these roadmaps serve as a table of contents for judicial officers, which is invaluable when trial court rules do not provide for a table of contents.

§ 3 *A Compelling Narrative*

After an impactful introduction comes the fact section, which is designed to inform, persuade and keep the momentum. A statement of facts should present only the meaningful facts and only in the proper order, unadorned by chocolate and flowers. A persuasive narrative recounts the story with purpose and specificity. Each fact must serve a discrete purpose.

Persuasive writers prefer plain and simple words, and recruit vivid verbs and concrete nouns to do the heavy lifting. They distrust adjectives and adverbs, so would never describe a hurricane as *inclement weather*, or lament a 25-mile backup as *congestion.* They provide the data and empower the readers to reach their own opinions, which the vivid verbs and concrete nouns should make obvious and inevitable.

I can disclose that judges gravitate to facts and detail over adjectives and generalized representations. Persuasive writers know that select detail makes their prose more interesting, persuasive and memorable. Detail inspires reader confidence, literally. Research has shown that detail improves a writer's credibility.

A study from December 2024 showed that people found memories more believable and trustworthy when they included specific details about what actually happened, compared to memories that only had vague or general descriptions.[181]

This example is pulled from the department of child safety's brief on appeal in support of the lower court's termination of father's parental rights:

> Child had a relationship with Father before his June 2015 incarceration, but Father demonstrated poor judgment and parenting skills. He arranged for Child to drink fruit juice from empty mini-liquor bottles and bought Child candy cigarettes.

But too much detail overloads readers, distracting them from what matters and impeding their path to comprehension.

So what's the right amount? Aim for between overloading the reader and oversimplifying the subject. Determine which facts are needed to prove a claim or defense. Pretend your reader is an educated layperson. A shorter fact section focuses the reader on important facts. Justice Benjamin Cardozo, among the pantheon of legal writers, advised lawyers to include "only the essential facts" and "avoid facts that're merely decorative or coincidental."[182] I concur. Say what must be said and no more.

There is an accuracy that defeats itself by the overemphasis of details.

—BENJAMIN CARDOZO[183]

Accuracy is paramount. As discussed in Chapter 7, Be Credible, writers who offer inaccurate facts will lose credibility with readers faster than ice cream melts in the Arizona desert. Readers proceed with suspicion, if at all—wondering what else is fudged.

Although the statement of facts must not contain argument, [it must] be designed to persuade. You advance that objective by your terminology, by your selection and juxtaposition of the facts, and by the degree of prominence you give to each. You will amplify the facts that suggest your desired outcome by placing them prominently in the narrative.

—JUSTICE ANTONIN SCALIA
& BRYAN GARNER[184]

EXERCISES

This exercise is for judicial writing. Trim these facts, pretending the defendant was convicted of one count of using a firearm in a drug crime and his conviction is on direct appeal.

> On December 11, 1990, officers of the Metropolitan Police Department executed a search warrant on a one-bedroom apartment at 2525 14th Street, N.E., in the District of Columbia. Upon entering the apartment, the officers found appellant seated on a small couch in the living room; they detained him while they searched the apartment. The search produced two ziplock bags containing a total of 15.7 grams of crack cocaine divided among 100 smaller ziplock bags, $500 in cash, empty ziplock bags, razor blades, and three loaded and operable pistols. Two of the guns were under the cushions of the couch on which appellant sat; the third was in a nightstand in the bedroom. The cocaine and the cash were in an air duct vent in the ceiling of the bedroom. In the drawer of a dresser in the bedroom, the officers found two birthday cards; appellant's name was on the envelope of one, and the other was for a "son," signed "Mr. and Mrs. B. G. Morris" and dated November 30, 1990. No address was on either. In a hallway closet, the officers found a laundry ticket dated December 3, 1990, and bearing

> the name "E. Morris." There were no identifiable fingerprints on any of these items. The officers arrested appellant, who was indicted on two counts: possession with intent to distribute in excess of five grams of cocaine base and using or carrying a firearm in relation to the possession offense.[185]

§ 4 Make Your Writing Inviting

I've been told that style has no place in academic and legal writing because it elevates form over substance, exposing an unserious writer. Rubbish. Writing is a visual and audio art. It catches the eye, steers the gaze and warms the ear. A persuasive writer accounts for the look and sound of their prose.

A. Style

A writing style is the distinctive cocktail of decisions made by a particular writer on issues of convention during the writing process. It captures the design of words and paragraphs, measuring how a point is made, not the point's meaning.

A writing style belongs to the writer and is distinctive, separating one writer from the next. Style can vary depending on the audience and objective, but not in the same document. An erratic, whimsical approach only confuses the reader and weakens your credibility. Whatever the venue, a writing style must never overshadow the merits or diminish the force of expression.

I'm a fan and proponent of the plain style, which works well in persuasive writing. The plain style aspires to distill the point into the fewest words, discarding adverbs and leaving only the point:

Plain Style	Classic Style
The truth is pure and simple.	The truth is rarely pure and never simple.[186]

Like music and painting, a writing style is created stroke by stroke, decision by decision. Let's turn to some of those decisions and see how persuasive writers approach them.

1. Variety

The ear demands variety. One step, pivot and weave. Make your paragraphs fresh with short, medium and long sentences. Be careful not to stack sentences of the same length because it's distracting and uninspiring. Vary the length of your sentences and paragraphs to please the eye and ear.

Let me show you what I mean. This paragraph is comprised entirely of three-word sentences and it induces a coma:

> Remember these words. Welcome to monotony. Monotony has arrived. This is slow. You are bored. I am too. It drones on. Three more words. Cut and paste. Hard to concentrate. Where am I? Welcome to monotony. Monotony has arrived.

This paragraph might look attractive with 13 parallel sentences, but it has the flair of a flip phone, the charm of a cardboard box—labored and monotonous, tired and stale. The human brain needs a varied presentation.

A glimmer of variety adds the missing spice:

> Me again. I mix things up here, and it creates a melody. The words sway this way and that, here and there. I use short sentences. Then I use medium-length sentences to explore an argument in greater depth. And sometimes, I will unleash a longer sentence, one that builds to a boil—the roll of the drums, the roar of an air horn—listen to me scream. This is important.

This paragraph varies the rhythm. It fuses long (29 words) and short sentences (two or three words) to create music that ends with emphasis. It uses punctuation and words to extend sentences, which build in pressure until the final jarring sentence.

Take this example from the antitrust lawsuit we read about earlier between 1-800-CONTACTS and its largest competitor:

> 1-800 has long fashioned itself as a champion of consumers and an outspoken advocate for open and robust competition. 1-800 has emphasized, in particular, the importance of informed consumers who understand their alternatives. Indeed, in its protracted battle with eye care practitioners and manufacturers, 1-800 often decried the conduct of entrenched business interests that zealously guarded their pecuniary self-interest at the expense of meaningful consumer choice and greater competition. It was all a ruse.

This paragraph varies the rhythm. Many say that antitrust law is boring, but this sentence fuses long (36 words) and short sentences (five words) to spark interest and attention.

By varying the length of your sentences and paragraphs, you veer from certitude to nuance and back. Short paragraphs give the reader a chance to catch their breath and process what has come and gone.

> *Writing is not different from life—you want variety, you want refreshment, and you want balance.*
>
> —Alice Walker[187]

2. Blank Space

Academic and legal writers hardly ever leave enough space between their paragraphs.

The Japanese have a word called *ma*, which celebrates empty or negative space as invisible energy, describing that space as necessary to breathe, feel and connect. *Ma* teaches that words draw their power from silence and emphasis on what remains.

Zen prizes this same quality. Blank space represents the foundation of three Zen arts: gardening, ink-wash painting and flower arrangement. Zen teaches that space exists to be safeguarded, not filled.

Blank space is necessary to persuade because the human eye collects data by registering light. Without blank space, a text feels cluttered and uninviting. Something exists only in relation to nothing.

When a paragraph runs across multiple pages, it discourages the reader from moving forward. Who can sympathize with this unlucky chap? This text looks as inviting as dental surgery. Add blank space to legal and persuasive writing to make it easier for the reader to read rather than ignore your words.

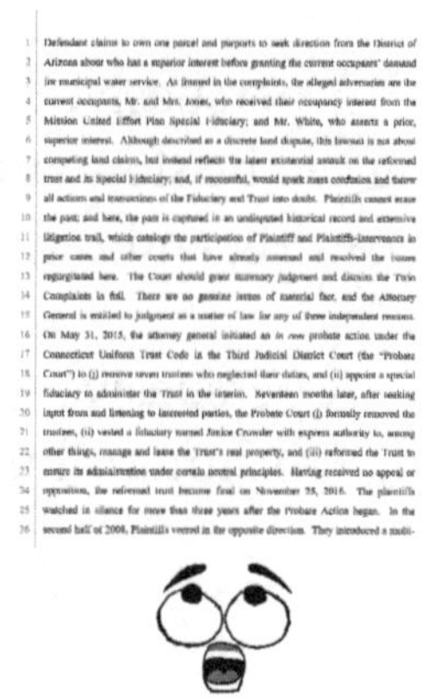

Defendant claims to own one parcel and purports to seek direction from the District of Arizona about who has a superior interest before granting the current occupants' demand for municipal water service. As framed in the complaints, the alleged adversaries are the current occupants, Mr. and Mrs. Jones, who received their occupancy interest from the Mission United Effort Plan Special Fiduciary; and Mr. White, who asserts a prior, superior interest. Although described as a discrete land dispute, this lawsuit is not about competing land claims, but instead reflects the latest existential assault on the reformed trust and its Special Fiduciary; and, if successful, would spark mass confusion and throw all actions and transactions of the Fiduciary and Trust into doubt. Plaintiffs cannot erase the past; and here, the past is captured in an undisputed historical record and extensive litigation trail, which catalogs the participation of Plaintiff and Plaintiffs-Intervenors in prior cases and other courts that have already assessed and resolved the issues regurgitated here. The Court should grant summary judgment and dismiss the Twin Complaints in full. There are no genuine issues of material fact, and the Attorney General is entitled to judgment as a matter of law for any of three independent reasons. On May 31, 2015, the attorney general initiated an *in rem* probate action under the Connecticut Uniform Trust Code in the Third Judicial District Court (the "Probate Court") to (i) remove seven trustees who neglected their duties, and (ii) appoint a special fiduciary to administer the Trust in the interim. Seventeen months later, after seeking input from and listening to interested parties, the Probate Court (i) formally removed the trustees, (ii) vested a fiduciary named Janice Crowder with express authority to, among other things, manage and lease the Trust's real property, and (iii) reformed the Trust to ensure its administration under certain neutral principles. Having received no appeal or opposition, the reformed trust became final on November 25, 2016. The plaintiffs watched in silence for more than three years after the Probate Action began. In the second half of 2008, Plaintiffs veered in the opposite direction. They introduced a multi-

3. Tone

Tone represents the personal attitude a writer brings to their work. It comes from the way ideas are expressed—logical, conventional, clinical, academic, emotional, objective, subjective, intimate, distant, serious and humorous. All writing has a tone. It turns on word choice, viewpoint, grammar and formality.

Persuasive writers calibrate their tone to meet the task at hand. A conversational tone is pitch-perfect for someone who must describe and argue abstract concepts.

An emotional tone is tricky. When emotion is relevant to the elements of a claim or defense, it should be conveyed. But a disproportionate amount of emotion may be unhelpful and even destroy your credibility.

4. Sound

A persuasive sentence accounts for sound. Writing can be slow and dull and put a reader to sleep, or it can zig and zag and hold a reader's attention.

A persuasive writer tests the sound of their writing. Although humans read with their eyes, they hear the words too. Think of the Morgan Freeman memes, where his picture is presented with an excerpt of text. Most readers hear the text in Morgan's distinctive voice. We hear the words because our visual, speech and auditory centers are bound together in the reading brain. Persuasive prose is fine-tuned using rhythm and alliteration.

Rhythm arises from the cadence of your prose. A pleasant rhythm springs from punctuation, sentence length, the number of syllables in each chosen word, the stress patterns of words, and the placement of words and punctuation to create breaks and pauses. This phenomenon is like music, except the rhythm in music is more pronounced due to bassists and drummers, who keep the beat and empower the band members to pursue alternative but agreeable agendas.

Persuasive writing begs for rhythm. Great oral advocates develop a rhythm to command your attention and move your mind. And yet, many eloquent oral advocates ditch their love of rhythm when it comes to written communication, insisting it's only the stuff of poets and rock stars. That is wrong and it ignores the cognitive relationship between rhythm and persuasion.

Readers are more likely to accept an argument as truth when accompanied by rhythm and rhyme. The psychologist Daniel Kahneman discovered that aphorisms "were judged more insightful when they rhymed than when they did not."[188]

New writers and professionals are too focused on the meaning of their sentences to worry how they sound. They look straight past the ear to the brain.

If you want to test or improve your rhythm, then read your drafts aloud. Listen for passages with a monotonous rhythm. Better yet, have Gwyneth Paltrow or Barack Obama read your stuff aloud. Software developers offer programs that read your stuff aloud in the voices of celebrities and politicians. I love Speechify.

> *The test of a sentence is: Does it sound right? The basic elements of language are physical: the noise words make, the sounds and silences that make the rhythms marking their relationships. Both the meaning and the beauty of the writing depend on these sounds and rhythms.*
>
> —Justice Clarence Thomas[189]

Alliteration is the repetition of the same first sound in closely positioned words. Justice Benjamin Cardozo treasured "the mnemonic power of alliteration," which facilitates pace and improves clarity.[190] Persuasive writers aim to reduce friction between them and readers in the communication process. But take caution, a legal brief looks like slapstick comedy when these tools are overused, distracting the reader from what matters.

5. *Parallelism*

Persuasive prose is sculpted with parallel balance and symmetry. Parallelism is a technique that uses word forms, phrases or clauses more than once in a sentence or paragraph. It resembles an echo—the same or similar words and phrases are positioned in the same part of a sentence to create balance, to produce pleasant rhythms and to emphasize a point.

But watch out. When used in parallel form, each word, phrase or clause must have the same grammatical form. Words:

The women tried running, weights and biking. (NO)	The women tried running, weightlifting and biking. (YES)

Phrases:

We read the briefs, discussed the case in conference and the unanimous decision was to affirm. (NO)	We read the briefs, discussed the case in conference and unanimously decided to affirm. (YES)

Elements joined by a coordinating conjunction must also be parallel:

Love and being married go together. (NO)	Love and marriage go together. (YES)

A parallel construction is also required after the words *than* and *as*:

Renting an apartment can be more expensive than the acquisition of a home. (NO)	Renting an apartment can be more expensive than acquiring a home. (YES)

For sentences with a series of prepositional phrases, the phrase need not be repeated when it starts each phrase.

Courts make decisions based on the law, on the facts and on the equities. (NO)	Courts make decisions based on the law, facts and equities. (YES)

6. Purposeful Repetition and Elegant Variation

Persuasive writers purposefully repeat hand-picked words or phrases to create emphasis and improve comprehension. When encountered more than once, readers are more likely to understand, appreciate and remember a complex idea.[191]

A cousin of purposeful repetition is elegant variation. Elegant variation happens when one thing is expressed in more than one way. For instance, pronouns may be varied and an indefinite article may be changed to a definite article:

- Maya brought her work home. She had to finish it by tomorrow.
- I bought a house. The house had a leak.
- Robert and Sarah married in 2020. They had known each other for over a decade. The couple divorced in 2022.

Elegant variation keeps your prose fresh, but don't overdo it. Like most grammar, it works best when invisible.

B. Rhetorical Devices

In an earlier chapter, we tackled three rhetorical devices: analogies, metaphors and similes. Here we tackle rhetorical devices that hinge on sound.

When so used, rhetorical devices are word patterns that create rhythm designed to stress a point, evoke a reaction and forge aesthetic appeal. Each has a distinct pattern that emphasizes what you mean, helping the reader connect related ideas. Studies have shown that rhetorical figures are persuasive because ideas articulated in verse are more likely to be accepted as true.[192]

A word of warning. Like most good things, the rhetorical figures described in this chapter will backfire if misused or overused.

1. Epizeuxis

Epizeuxis is the simplest rhetorical device. It repeats a word three times in quick succession and without interruption. This device is used in many languages. It stresses a particular thought or idea through repetition and rhythmic effect:

> Location, location, location.[193]
> Words, words, words alone.[194]

2. Anaphora

Anaphora repeats the same words or phrases to start successive sentences or clauses. It builds momentum and leaves a hammering effect.

> *Courage* is what it takes to stand up and speak. *Courage* is also what it takes to sit down and listen.[195]

This device is designed to describe something that happened several times or in several places:

> *We shall fight* on the beaches. *We shall fight* on the landing grounds. *We shall fight* in the fields, and in the streets, *we shall fight* in the hills. *We shall* never surrender.[196]

Anaphora is prevalent in persuasive writing because it creates an urgency. When I think of *anaphora*, I think of Dr. Martin Luther King on the steps of the Lincoln Memorial in 1963 when he used *I Have a Dream* as a chorus and call to action. Dr. King started eight consecutive sentences with that timeless, venerated phrase.

3. *Conduplicatio*

Conduplicatio repeats the same words or phrases, like *anaphora*, but those words and phrases appear at or near the start of a sentence and are separated by other words. Common in persuasive writing, it works well to connect ideas, and to announce, amplify or explain a theme or statement:

> The U.S. Supreme Court anticipated and rejected this very *same* argument in *Glossip*, where the *same* attorneys *here* challenged the *same* three drug protocols *here* based on the *same* incompatible argument *here*.

4. *Epanalepsis*

Epanalepsis uses the same word or phrase at the start and finish of one or more sentences. It fuses a sentence together. It creates a circular action that revisits the original point for emphasis. When repeated, the repeated word completes the thought:

> Control, control, you must learn control.[197]

> Ambition must be made to counteract ambition.[198]

5. *Epistrophe*

Epistrophe is the opposite of *anaphora*. It repeats a word or phrase at or near the end of successive sentences or clauses.

> The wrongs which we seek to condemn and punish have been so calculated, so malignant, and so devastating, that civilization *cannot* tolerate *their being* ignored, because it *cannot* survive *their being* repeated.[199]

6. *Chiasmus*

Chiasmus is best described as a grammatical mirror. It reverses the grammatical structure of successive clauses or sentences, and is often used to rebut or argue against a point by reversing it. It has many famous examples. President John F. Kennedy used it in his inaugural address:

> Ask not what your country can do for you,
> but what you can do for your country.[200]

Justice Robert Jackson used it to stress the finality of the U.S. Supreme Court:

> We are not final because we are infallible, but
> we are infallible only because we are final.[201]

7. Isocolon

The word *isocolon* comes from the Greek words *isos* and *kolon*, which mean *equal* and *clause*. An *isocolon* happens when a sentence or series of sentences use two or more phrases of *similar* structure and length.

Julius Caesar and J.F.K. shared at least one thing in common—they both loved the *isocolon*.

> I came, I saw, I conquered.[202]

> Let every nation know, whether it wishes us well or ill, that we shall pay any price, bear any burden, meet any hardship, support any friend, oppose any foe, in order to assure the survival and the success of liberty.[203]

C. Humor

Persuasive writers use microdoses of good-natured humor to connect and persuade the reader.

Take this example from Judge Barry Silverman of the Ninth Circuit who found himself writing the dissent in a thorny appeal to decide whether inmates possess a constitutional right to procreate.[204] An Arizona inmate in prison for life sued the government for a declaration that he enjoyed a civil right to impregnate his wife by mail. The majority found the inmate possessed that constitutional right. Silverman disagreed: "This is a seminal case in more ways than one [because] the majority simply does not accept the fact that there are certain downsides to being confined in prison," including "the interference with a normal family life." Silverman acknowledged the Eighth Amendment prohibits the government from exacting cruel and usual punishment, but he stressed that it does not establish "a constitutional right to procreate from prison via FedEx."

Judge Silverman had the final word. The Ninth Circuit later reexamined the case en banc, discarded the majority opinion and adopted Silverman's view. But tread carefully—humor backfires when improper or overdone.

EXERCISES

Read the following passage and circle all uses of parallelism:

> My style will not be at all florid; my expressions will be simple as the truth. Classic style is in its own view clear and simple as the truth. It adopts the stance that its purpose is presentation; its motive, disinterested truth. Successful presentation consists of aligning language with truth, and the test of this alignment is clarity and simplicity. The idea that presentation is successful when language is aligned with truth implies that truth can be known; truth needs no argument but only accurate presentation; the reader is competent to recognize truth; the symmetry between writer and reader allows the presentation to follow the model of conversation; a natural language is sufficient to express truth; and the writer knows the truth before he puts it into language.[205]

§ 5 Mindful Citation

Persuasive writers favor mindful citation. They supply targeted legal authority to support their arguments, preview major authorities with informative parentheticals, and direct their readers to the page and paragraph of each authority. They do not overwhelm the reader with string citations for no-brainer points, like the standard for summary judgment, and do not use legal citations as transitions to start consecutive paragraphs.

Persuasive writers craft well-engineered arguments with factual and legal authority at structural points. By structural points, I mean the facts and elements required to prove or disprove a claim and win the case. Think of a bridge. Each load-bearing column represents an element of a claim or defense. If any column falls, the bridge collapses.

Surplus authorities and string citations are generally not persuasive. That you've found seven cases that describe the elements for a breach of contract might interest historians but not the readers of your brief. Many lawyers think string citations add heft and persuasive value. Not so. Consider this string citation of judges who abhor string citations:

> String citations are ineffective and distracting. *See* Hon. John M. Duhe Jr., Judges on Briefing Today, 8 Scribes J. Legal Writing 1, 7 (2001–2002) ("Nor does it convince me for the writer to string out every cite he can find to support a point. A single, well-reasoned precedent is enough."); *see also* Hon. Arthur Gilbert, *id.* at 9 ("If one citation will do, a string of them will detract more than help

it."); Hon. Harold A. Kuskin, *id.* at 17 ("Multiple footnotes, string citations, citations from foreign jurisdictions that are marginally relevant, and 'learned' discussions of legal principles not in dispute are all boring, distracting, and ineffective."); Hon. E. Norman Veasey, *id.* at 25 ("If there is only weak authority for an argument, long string cites will not successfully disguise that fact."); Hon. William C. Whitbeck, *id.* at 26 ("[C]iting 'as much law as possible' is a truly dumb idea. It is, of course, the relevant law that is important, and string citations to every published case touching on the subject not only are aesthetically displeasing, but also make the judge's job harder. This is not a good idea if the brief-writer actually wants to win."); Hon. Roger J. Miner, Twenty-Five "Dos" for Appellate Brief Writers, 3 SCRIBES J. LEGAL WRITING 19, 24 (1992) ("Where there is one authoritative case in point, don't give six. Ban all string citations.").

A single, on-point case is far more effective than a string of marginal authorities. To exude confidence and enhance communication, pick the seminal or most persuasive case and stick with it.

And yet, string citations might be proper in limited circumstances to achieve a particular end. Most commonly, they are used to cite expansive acceptance. A writer might, for instance, want to explain that all federal circuits have reached the same conclusion on a particular issue. RULE NUMBER ONE

Parentheticals are persuasive. Explain why the case matters; use parentheticals to tell the reader what's important about a case or secondary authority. Craft short and informative parentheticals. Spend time on them because the reader is more likely to read a parenthetical and never read a case.

Pin cites are a courtesy (if not compelled by local rules), including page and paragraph numbers when available. The reader expects and welcomes this shortcut because it saves time. Readers are less likely to read an authority when pin cites are not given.

Avoid the nasty habit of using citations as transitions. Do not start six successive paragraphs with a full cite. By starting each paragraph with an unprimed abstraction, the reader suffers and will either fall asleep or grab the next document.

§ 6 Mindful Footnotes

Footnotes—little dogs yapping
at the heels of the text.

—William James[206]

Footnotes are not compelling. They are a disconnected way to impart a connected thought. They distract readers who must pause and twice redirect their gaze, first to the footnote and then back to the text. When readers lose their place or train of thought, they must find where they left off.

Footnotes hamper the narrative flow. Too many writers use footnotes as storage space for less important points they lacked the courage to delete. Briefs and opinions are less readable and less persuasive when peppered with clumsy footnotes.

Justices Stephen Breyer and Arthur Goldberg refused to use footnotes. In an interview for the U.S. Supreme Court's internal employee newsletter, *The Docket Sheet*, Breyer lamented the use of footnotes in legal writing: "I believe most footnotes are distracting. The purpose of a citation in a court argument is not to prove what your source was but to add to the argument. If it doesn't add to the argument, don't put it in. So I place citations in the text."[207]

§ 7 Mindful Block Quotes

Limit your block quotes. Long block quotes are rarely necessary or persuasive. A far superior alternative is to extract and weave. The writer first extracts the key words or phrases from the source, and then weaves them into his own words—with quotation marks and attribution.

Long quotes without an introduction are disconnected and ineffective. If unavoidable, introduce a block quote with a summary of its significance.

RULE NUMBER ONE

And yet, block quotes may be essential for transparency. For instance, before interpreting statutes and regulations, you should include a quote of the full relevant sections. Never paraphrase a statute, at least at first, because the judge wonders what's missing.

§ 8 *Mindful Lists*

Persuasive writers offer lists to furnish the reader concrete, no-nonsense direction. When making a list, they place the shortest, simplest item first (fewest words, least complex) and the hardest item last (most words, most complex). When the first point is long and hard, readers are discouraged and lose their balance.[208]

Psychologists advise that writers limit their lists to five or fewer items because working memory is limited. Shorter lists are more readable and increase clarity, focus and comprehension.[209] Lists make an argument skimmable.

A list of three items, in particular, resonates at the end of a sentence:

> Defendant Collins traveled to Las Vegas to meet his mother, where he was arrested for drugs, murder and unpaid parking tickets.

After all, three is the magic number. Most popular music relies on three chords; jokes have a setup, reiteration and punchline. A list of three builds rhythm, creating and then resolving tension. A list of four is diffuse and bloated; five or more is unruly.

§ 9 *Mindful Punctuation*

When face to face, speakers pause and raise or lower the tone of their voice to make a point. So too in writing. A persuasive writer deploys punctuation and spacing to guide readers to a particular destination, turning this:

> Persuasivepunctuationiswelcomingclearand-spareitdirectsandmovesthereadersfromone-wordsentenceandparagraphtothenextea-singthereadingpathtoprocessandrecallyoura-rgument

. . . into this:

> Persuasive punctuation is welcoming, clear and spare. It directs and moves the readers from one word, sentence and paragraph to the next—easing the reading path to process and recall your argument.

Punctuation marks were first concocted to mark pauses for public speakers. Each mark (commas, semicolons, colons, periods) indicated a pause of different length. By some accounts, the pause for a period was four times longer than the pause for a comma. But printers and grammarians later repurposed these and other marks as tools of semantic understanding.

Punctuation has thus developed to serve two overlapping purposes—(1) regulating the reading voice and (2) signposting grammatic relationships.

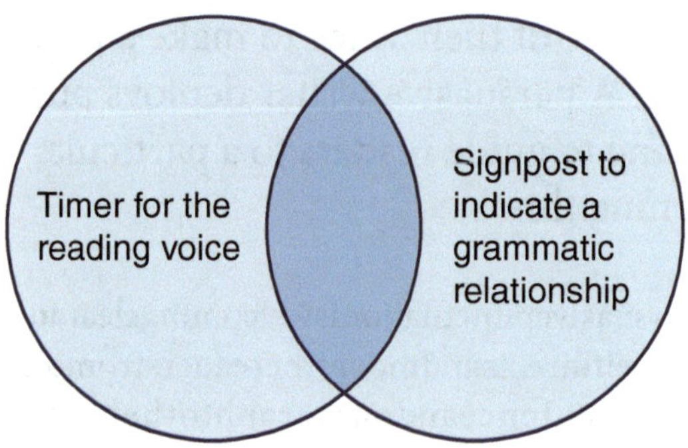

Most debates over punctuation arise from this distinction, including the timeless fight over the Oxford comma, discussed below.

Punctuate with care. With a dash here and a dot there, punctuation makes a big difference. Watch for meaning that hinges on punctuation. Indeed, punctuation has the power to change the meaning of identical words in the identical order:

A woman, without her man, is nothing.
A woman: without her, man is nothing.

I'm sorry I love you.
I'm sorry; I love you.

Persuasive writers punctuate for clarity and emphasis; they know how to punctuate for special effect, and how to create rhythm, cadence and momentum.

A. Period

A period is used to end declarative (statements) and imperative (commands) sentences; it also signifies abbreviations and initials.

Writers have long sparred over how many spaces should follow a period. This passionate debate has engendered substantial animosity and these disparate groups continue to duel for supremacy. Some writers insist that one space reduces the need for eye movements and thus saves time and effort; other writers insist that two spaces make the text easier to read and more attractive. One study showed that readers read slightly faster when two spaces follow a sentence.[210] When releasing opinions and memorandum decisions, I prefer two spaces because readers consume text in chunks.

B. Comma

The comma is a slender and pliable mark that does different things: it demarcates words in a series, flanks parenthetical and non-restrictive elements and signals a brief pause for clarity.

The modern comma might be the product of capitalism, invented by a Venetian printer in the late 1400s. Born in 1449, Aldus Manutius rose to international prominence as a printer in Venice. And from all accounts, he was a good businessman who understood economics. When Manutius opened his business, the comma was marked by a full forward slash or /. To grow his marginal profit, Manutius devised a new comma that required less ink. Manutius believed a less pronounced mark could do the same job, and the modern comma was born.[211]

Commas are vital in longer sentences but hard to install because they are expected to unscramble an unfolding thought. Long, lucid and graceful sentences are impossible unless writers are comfortable with commas.

A single comma may carry the meaning of a sentence.

I went to the lawnmower museum, alone.

When misplaced or omitted, a missing comma can be deadly.

Let's hunt, daddy.
Let's hunt daddy.

All grammar and punctuation demand the reader's attention and brain power. The comma is no exception. Commas should not be overused or underused because it distracts and confuses the reader.

1. Oxford Version

A serial or Oxford comma introduces a conjunction (and, or) and the final item in a series of three or more:

Emotion defeats reason when the issue turns to religion, politics, and the Oxford comma.

The Oxford comma is controversial—even at Oxford, where a schism formed between the Oxford University Press and Oxford University's public affairs department.[212] The Oxford University Press had required the serial comma as its house style since 1893, when, in 2011, Oxford University's public affairs department announced the mark would not be used unless necessary for clarity. The backlash was immediate and predictable:

Are you people insane?

The Oxford comma is what separates us from the animals.

—TWEET FROM @ED3
(DECEMBER 2, 2011)

Where you stand on the Oxford comma depends on how you hear and see the comma—either as a device to regulate the reading voice or indicate a grammatic relationship. On one end, readers who hear the comma as a mark to regulate the reading voice are unlikely to use the Oxford comma, believing it unnecessarily spoils both pace and momentum. On the other end, readers who see the comma as a signpost for grammatic relationships embrace the Oxford comma.

Most pedants and grammatical guides favor the Oxford comma because it can be trusted to clarify any ambiguity that might (or might not) arise. Most newspapers and magazines favor omitting the Oxford comma for its brevity (it requires one less character) and the marginal cost of ink on paper (before the digital world emerged). Associated Press reporters are directed to use the Oxford comma if leaving it out creates ambiguity or confusion.[213]

A persuasive writer accounts for the reader's journey, pedants be damned, interested only in reader comprehension and recall. No punctuation mark deserves absolute fidelity. The only excuse for an absolutism on the Oxford comma is a lack of confidence or time. Oxford-comma absolutists either don't trust themselves to use the serial comma when necessary, or refuse to spend the time needed to distinguish between when it's necessary and unnecessary.

The Oxford comma is like sunscreen to me: applied as needed. I use a serial comma when necessary to avoid confusion. For instance, the Oxford comma has no value here:

Mike finds joy in cooking, jogging and his dog.	Mike finds joy in cooking, jogging, and his dog.

But the Oxford comma is absolutely necessary here because *Steel Magnolias* and *Caddy Shack* are not horror flicks:

He watched two horror movies, *Steel Magnolias* and *Caddy Shack.*	He watched two horror movies, *Steel Magnolias*, and *Caddy Shack*.

An Oxford comma is also essential here unless you're tight with the frontman for the Rolling Stones and his pet:

We invited my best friends, Mick Jagger and his dog.	We invited my best friends, Mick Jagger, and his dog.

And don't think that absolute fidelity to the Oxford comma will avoid all hiccups:

I hugged her dad, a swimsuit model and four jugglers.	I hugged her dad, a swimsuit model, and four jugglers.

The meaning of the first sentence is clear—I hugged six people. By adding an Oxford comma, we lose one guest and her father becomes a swimsuit model.

I include serial commas for cadence and parallel rhythm, too.

Writing rules are everywhere—in every profession, every law firm, and every government agency.

Summary: When an Oxford comma is essential to preserve meaning and avoid confusion, it must always be used. But it need not be used when unnecessary to preserve meaning or avoid confusion.

In full disclosure, my opinion is not shared by any current U.S. Supreme Court justice, so take it with a handful of salt.[214]

C. The Colon

A persuasive writer uses the colon to introduce a list or explanation and to emphasize what follows. It guides the reader from general to specific:

> The stewardess suffered from debilitating pain as she traveled three continents: Asia, North America and South America.

D. The Semicolon

Aldus Manutius invented the modern comma, but did you know he invented the semicolon, too? The man was prolific. Manutius invented the semicolon to create a pause that was longer than a comma but shorter than a period.[215]

Semicolons are cast in the role of a comma and seven conjunctions—for, and, nor, but, or, yet, so. I use this punctuation mark to compare and contrast two items or points.

> Mike was American; John was French.
>
> He was late; she was early.

Semicolons are frequently used in legal writing to demarcate parts of long lists when a comma is not enough.

E. Em Dash

An em dash is dynamic—it signals an abrupt pause and casts a spotlight on the words that follow. It may create emphasis and anticipation:

> He was armed—seized with 21 handguns, four grenades and a Russian tank.

An em dash also works well for parenthetical expressions that demand a greater pause than the comma, and deserve more emphasis than the parentheses.

> His accomplishments—the Nobel Prize, the Booker Prize, the Pulitzer Prize—speak for themselves.

> The patient's illness—first physical, then mental—perplexed the medical staff.

An em dash also signals a break in speech caused by hesitation or uncertainty, or to show that speech is broken off entirely.

> I don't want you—I mean, I never did.

And yet, too many dashes ruin your writing, making it look and read like Morse code, permanently interrupting itself.

F. The Hyphen

A hyphen is used to join two or more words forming an adjective to place before a noun. A hyphen can be the difference between eating a nice meal and being the meal:

Man-eating shark.

Man eating shark.

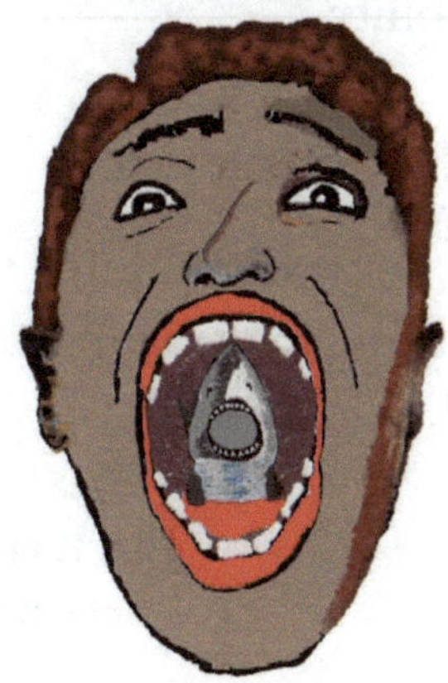

G. Parentheticals, Question Marks, Quotation Marks and Exclamation Points

When writers want to insert a running commentary or argue in the alternative, they may cordon off the words with parentheticals:

> Even if Plaintiff had standing (she does not), she cannot prove the required elements of his claim.

A question mark announces a question. It comes equipped with its own voice inflection. Quotation marks are used to identify quotes or idioms.

> Wanna see my guns?
> Wanna see my "guns"?

Exclamation points have no role in persuasive writing unless they appear in a quoted source. They are distracting and will impair the writer's credibility.

H. Contractions

A contraction joins two words with an apostrophe, using fewer words and letters to make the same point.

> That is against the law.
> That's against the law.

Contractions are conversational. When used right, they make legal writing more approachable and less intimidating. But many able judges swear that contractions have no place in legal writing. I think that's silly. Judges should strive to be understood. And like Stephen King said, "Language does not always have to wear a tie and lace-up shoes."[216]

Don't get me wrong. It's easy to overdo. Too many contractions will backfire—lulling your reader into a sense of malaise and draining the heft of your prose. But a thoughtfully placed contraction in formal persuasive writing is the bomb! Yes, I said it. The bomb. It hits you unexpectedly, imbued with a colloquial quality that softens the subject matter.

I. Capitalization

Persuasive writers do not use all-caps unless it's a business name, part of an acronym, quoting something in all-caps or required by law (warranties). For what it's worth, an MIT experiment found that comprehension is not improved with all capital letters.[217]

> Punctuation marks are like music instruments. Each produces a distinct sound. Forge a rhythm and cadence that appeals to the reader.
>
> *Meditation*

§ 10 Mindful Typography

Reading is burdensome when the font is hard to read. Persuasive writers account for font type, font size and spacing when drafting and redrafting their work product. They use a legible font when permissible, which requires little effort from the writer, but substantially improves reading speed. According to one study, reading speed increased 35 percent depending on the font used.[218]

A less formal study found readers are more likely to believe text in legible font. Of six common fonts, it found writers are most credible when writing in Baskerville font; least credible when writing in Georgia font.[219]

Calibri is the default standard in Word, but superior fonts are available. The U.S. Supreme Court publishes opinions in Century Schoolbook font and requires lawyers to use the same. Different courts require different fonts. My court uses Book Antiqua.

Avoid bold and italics unless it helps. A persuasive writer relies on the words and sentences themselves to generate emphasis; no glitter or makeup is necessary. Typographical emphasis loses its power when overused.

CHAPTER 7
BE CREDIBLE

1 Honest
2 Connect and Concede
3 Accurate and Responsive
4 Respectful

Of prime importance, a brief should be trustworthy. If authorities are inaccurately described, the judge will lose confidence in the reliability of the brief and its author; if the judge reads on at all, she will do so with a skeptical eye.

—Justice Ruth Bader Ginsburg[220]

Persuasive writers earn a reputation for honesty, accuracy and responsiveness among colleagues and in the courts. A fine reputation is not earned in one day or one year; it is cultivated and preserved over the course of your career.

§ 1 Honest

There is a vague popular belief that lawyers are necessarily dishonest. . . . Let no young man choosing the law for a calling for a moment yield to the popular belief—resolve to be honest at all events; and if in your own judgment you cannot be an honest lawyer, resolve to be honest without being a lawyer.

—President Abraham Lincoln[221]

Trust is an essential ingredient to persuasion. Readers are more open-minded when they know, like or respect the writer. According to Daniel Kahneman, readers enjoy a feeling of cognitive ease when reading a writer they trust.[222]

Never play fast and loose with the facts or law. Never intentionally lie or carelessly misrepresent. If you do either, you'll gain a reputation for deception and slovenliness. And that reputation is infectious—it spreads among the bench and bar.

Honesty is also vital in the legal profession; it ensures fair trials, protects the integrity of the legal system and builds trust between parties. Lawyers must be honest with clients, the court and other lawyers. If lawyers are dishonest, the whole system collapses.

Trust is lost by disassembly or conveying false information—not just intentionally but even carelessly; by mischaracterizing precedent to suit your case; by making arguments that could appeal only to the stupid or uninformed; by ignoring rather than confronting whatever weighs against your case.

—Justice Antonin Scalia
& Bryan Garner[223]

§ 2 Connect and Concede

Persuasive writers know how and when to brandish weakness in the larger battle for truth and justice. The power of concession has been touted since at least the 14th century when François de La Rochefoucauld, author and moralist, advised: "We admit to small faults to persuade others that we have no great ones."[224] President Abraham Lincoln was likewise known to concede the inessential when necessary to prevail on the essential.

Many advocates think they cannot concede an inch, convinced they're paid to defend all incoming fire. That is wrong. A wee bit of vulnerability gains the trust and even admiration of the audience. Better still if the concession is inconsequential, covering facts or law that are inessential to your success. Equipped with credibility, the advocates can then pivot to their stronger points.

§ 3 *Accurate and Responsive*

Persuasive writers are accurate. They never offer bad information or misstate the law because it has consequences. It saps the reader's confidence, drawing their attention from your point to your motivations.

Persuasive writers are also responsive. Many writers think they can run from bad arguments or hard issues. Not so. When advocates ignore an issue or argument, the silence is deafening. The issue or argument does not go away, only your chance to frame and discuss it. If you have no answer for an issue or argument, concede that fact and push forward to more fruitful points.

§ 4 Respectful

A claim stated moderately is more likely to be taken thoughtfully. Avoid background noise, which are words and phrases that distract the reader from what matters. Disrespectful prose is rooted in animus, motivated by a twisted impression of the legal profession and unleashed by unclear writers who cannot express a point or denigrate for kicks.

Steer clear of personal attacks and name-calling. And watch for adjectives and adverbs, which moonlight as background noise.

Does this move your heart or mind? The writer might intend to convey the intensity of his feelings, but the court is distracted and likely annoyed.

If inescapable, the persuasive writer quotes another source for the background noise, which creates the illusion of distance between him and the noise. For example:

> Attorneys must never ignore the record or law on appeal. *See Gonzalez-Servin v. Ford Motor Co.*, 662 F.3d 931, 934 (7th Cir. 2011) ("The ostrich is a noble animal, but not a proper model for an appellate advocate.") (J. Posner).

Summary: All advocates are born with an untarnished reputation. Guard it zealously.

Full of sound and fury,
Signifying nothing.

—William Shakespeare
(MacBeth)[225]

Angry people are not always wise.

—Jane Austen[226]

Chapter 8
BE A READER AND WRITER

1 Read More
2 Write More

§ 1 *Read More*

Neuroimaging studies show a strong correlation between reading and writing, likely because these disparate functions rely on shared skills and overlapping brain regions.[227]

You must read. Lawyers who don't read outside the profession never develop the deep, nimble vocabulary that distinguishes good and bad writers.

Studies in 2006 and 2000 found that reading strengthens writing.[228] Writing improves from reading because the writer is exposed to diverse writing styles, vocabulary, sentence structures and narrative techniques. What is read becomes a model for language use, structure and style.

As you read, so will you write. If you read nothing but pulp and tabloid newspapers, you will write like them.

—Justice Antonin Scalia & Bryan Garner[229]

But the prose must be good, modern prose that embraces the virtue of clarity. Read George Orwell and Ernest Hemingway. Asked by a reporter how lawyers could improve their timeless reputation for poor writing, Judge Richard Posner said to read Orwell and imitate his prose, which he described as "very clear, very impressive, articulate, fresh, humorous, and nontechnical."[230]

Read, read, read. Read everything—
trash, classics, good and bad,
and see how they do it. Just like
a carpenter who works as an
apprentice and studies the master.
Read! You'll absorb it. Then write.
If it's good, you'll find out. If it's
not, throw it out of the window.

—William Faulkner[231]

§ 2 *Write More*

You must write. Like judgment and confidence, your writing improves with experience. Gain experience and your writing will improve.

Emulate your favorite writers. Read and reverse-engineer their prose.[232] Joan Didion did it. She admired Ernest Hemingway for his "perfect sentences," which resembled "smooth rivers, clear water over granite, no sinkholes." And so, when Didion was 15 or 16 years old, she "would type out his stories to learn how the sentences worked."[233] Find what you like and break it down.

> *If you want to be a writer, you must do two things above all others: read a lot and write a lot. If you don't have time to read, you don't have the time (or the tools) to write. Simple as that.*
>
> —Stephen King[234]

CHAPTER 9
BE METICULOUS AND REWRITE

1 STRUCTURE
2 LENGTH
3 CLARITY
4 ACCURACY AND TYPOS
5 FEEDBACK

I have never thought of myself as a good writer. But I'm one of the world's great rewriters.

—JAMES MICHENER[235]

Bad legal writers write fast and do not rewrite. They either do not account for the audience or think all readers are fungible. Writing is easy for them and they produce unclear and unpersuasive writing at a record pace.

I know many good writers who write and rewrite simultaneously (I do), but that does not replace the need for a careful revision on the back end. Only after the first draft can the writer redirect his cognitive gaze to matters of grammar and grace. Writers need time and distance from their first draft to grab the largest axe.

When your first draft is done, set it aside and return with a refreshed mind—a quick reboot to create emotional detachment from an original creation. Then audit your draft for structure, length, clarity, coherence, accuracy and typographical error.

The only kind of writing is rewriting.

—Ernest Hemingway[236]

§ 1 Structure

Readers crave order and order needs structure, so persuasive writers revise for structure, ordering and reordering the facts and law of their argument until it flows. A document flows when the reader glides from one page to the next without circling back for missing information. For prose that flows, reading is a seamless exercise.

Structural defects in legal writing are like potholes on the road to persuasion. By revising for structure, writers bring coherence and order to their prose, ensuring the reader understands both sequence and logic.

To test the flow of their documents, persuasive writers underline the first six words or the first sentence of each paragraph and ask whether the underlined words accurately preview the paragraph. Do the underlined words tell the story? Are common words and themes underlined? Are related chunks of information treated in different locations? Can they be united?

To improve the flow of their documents, persuasive writers reread the first draft and answer these questions: Have they provided context? Have they introduced new information based on that context? Have they primed the reader for more? Have they kept related ideas together? Have they used topic sentences? Have they used transitions and do the transitions work? Have they reached and discussed each step in their logical analysis? Do their sentences, paragraphs and sections sensibly link one thought to the next? Do their paragraphs blend together into a coherent whole?

Test the aesthetics, too. Are there enough paragraph breaks? Are the sentences and paragraphs of different length? Is there enough blank space?

> *Let's speak of [rewriting] in terms of furniture arranging in your house. You put the sofa there. Then no, it might look better over here. Maybe it's the wrong sofa. Maybe we can put this sofa upstairs and then put this other different one here.*
>
> —Margaret Atwood[237]

§ 2 Length

The more paper you throw at us, the meaner we get, the more irritated and hostile we feel about verbosity, peripheral arguments and long footnotes.

—Judge Patricia Wald, D.C. Circuit[238]

If you respect the reader's time, reduce the footprint of your document. Yes, it's painful to delete. You devoted real time and mental energy to write those sentences or paragraphs, and you still intend to charge the client for them. But don't forget the audience (readers) and the objective (persuasion).

Persuasive writers never confuse length and merit. When I read long briefs, it's frequently because the writer has not spent the brain cells needed to decrease the length. I've seen an inverse relationship between page length and success. Shorter briefs are often the most persuasive. A utilitarian eye is imperative for persuasive writers. They reread and trim ruthlessly. They delete unnecessary, redundant and implied words. They delete unnecessary case law, secondary authorities, string cites and block quotes. They delete irrelevant procedure and events.

To decrease the length of their documents, persuasive writers reread the first draft and answer these questions: Are they being too wordy? Have they deleted gratuitous words and phrases, needless repetition and irrelevant material? Are they taking too long to say what they have to say? Have they deleted surplus adverbs and adjectives? Have they limited string citations and block quotes? Persuasive writers ask whether each paragraph is essential or inessential.

> *When your story is ready for rewrite, cut it to the bone. Get rid of every ounce of excess fat. This is going to hurt; revising a story down to the bare essentials is always a little like murdering children, but it must be done.*
>
> —Stephen King[239]

§ 3 *Clarity*

Clear writing happens with time and effort. As Jacques Barzun observed, "Simple English is no one's mother tongue. It has to be worked for."[240] Persuasive writers revise to erase any trace of ambiguity or indistinctness.

First drafts are less clear because clarity is achieved during the rewriting process. A running journal of one's thoughts is unlikely to be clear unless a writer revisits his work to rearrange the furniture.

To increase clarity, persuasive writers reread their first draft and answer these questions: Have they used headings to announce and emphasize the points? Have they deleted all fuzzy (hedges and nominalizations) and ornate words (legalese)? Have they deleted all throat-clearing phrases? Have they used concrete words to describe important points? Have they presented abstract points through metaphors and examples? How many words appear before the subject and verb in each sentence?

Persuasive writers ask what information is missing for readers to get the point. Have they mindfully defined terms? Have they trimmed the pomposity? Have they avoided double negatives? Have they misplaced any modifiers? Have they fallen victim to dual meanings and hedging? Do they rely too much on clichés or hackneyed phrases?

Delete every adverb and adjective before the noun, then restore only those adverbs and adjectives needed to understand the passage.

Every block of stone has
a statue inside it.

—Michelangelo[241]

§ 4 Accuracy and Typos

Proofread with a passion because accuracy is paramount for trust. It's not enough to present the most persuasive argument. When I see multiple, plain typographical errors, I furrow my brows and exhale crisply, nonplussed about the lack of attention to detail and language.

To test the accuracy of their documents, persuasive writers reread the first draft and answer these questions: Are all their facts accurate? They demand record support for all factual statements. Does their decisional law say what they say it says? Are the rules and statutes current? Do defined terms remain constant until the end? Are there missing words? Does the draft use proper tenses and plurals?

Persuasive writers are consistent on matters of abbreviation and capitalization. There are no excuses or alternatives when it comes to accuracy.

Check for spelling and typographical errors. Each year I receive briefs that misspell basic units of information, like the name of my court. In recent months, I received an opening brief titled Appellnt's Opening Briefe, which included a STATEMENT OF THE CASE HHISTORY AND ARGUIMENT. Not optimal. Your audience wonders why you didn't run a spellcheck and it saps their confidence. If quoting a source with such error, the writer adds [sic].

And even spellcheck is imperfect. Consider these real-world examples, which passed the spell-check gauntlet:

> The order found defendant had breached a contract with flatulent (fraudulent) intent.
>
> Wife filed for divorce after she caught Husband in bed with a power mower (paramour).
>
> At a time when Arizona is working to ensure access to justice in the legal desserts (deserts), the courts should not erect new barriers to be licensed.

Don't look sloppy. A judge might chuckle, but it won't help your cause. All documents must be cleansed of clerical and grammatical error.

§ 5 Feedback

When revising their work product, persuasive writers seek feedback from colleagues, friends and family. Yes, it's personal and not all criticism is good or well-intentioned. But persuasive writers have the confidence to listen to all ideas and accept the helpful ones. Listen to the audience and your prose will improve.

Summary: Persuasive prose is not crafted—it's recrafted and refined. You must revise because most first drafts are bloated, muddled and directionless. Like sculpting an unmolded blob of clay, it becomes meaningful only with time and attention.

Persuasive writers rehearse more to sound unrehearsed; they work hard to make it look easy. Maya Angelou and Judge Posner each confessed to hypocrisy on this front. Angelou told *The Paris Review*, "It must look easy, but it takes forever to get it to look easy."[242] And Posner conceded he goes through as many as 20 drafts to give his opinions "a casual, colloquial, and spontaneous appearance," adding, "I admit to hypocrisy in working so hard to give the appearance of effortlessness!"[243]

When a wise man is advised of his errors, he will reflect on and improve his conduct. When his misconduct is pointed out, a foolish man will not only disregard the advice but rather repeat the same error.

—The Buddha (568–488 BC)[244]

EXERCISES

Rewrite for clarity and concision.

1. For the purpose of orderly administration and the attainment of justice, certain rules are established. Any rule the enforcement of which results in a failure of justice should be carefully scrutinized and not blindly adhered to unless the abandonment of it will work more injustice than will follow if it be adhered to. (53)

2. I have tried to keep my language as simple as possible. Not only because Zen teaches and advocates the greatest economy of expression and because I have found that what I cannot say quite simply and without recourse to mystic jargon has not become sufficiently clear and concrete even to myself. (51)

3. In numerous cases over numerous decades, this Court has acknowledged that the First Amendment is applicable in situations in which the government, acting not as sovereign but as employer, places limits upon its workers' speech. (35)

4. The Seventh Circuit has indicated that any doubts concerning the arbitrability of claims should be resolved in favor of arbitration. *Rodgers v. Central Hospital*, 783 F.2d 485 (7th Cir. 1993). In *Rodgers*, the court stated: "The Arbitration Act establishes that as a matter of law any doubts concerning the scope of arbitrable issues and whether a claim should be arbitrated should be resolved in favor of arbitration." (67)

CHAPTER 10
CONCLUSION

One last chapter to summarize. Persuasive prose is clear. Persuasive writers realize that time and space separate them from their readers, so they craft their prose to answer questions that might be posed, easing the reader's path.

Persuasive prose knows the power of word choice. A persuasive writer knows and adores plenty of words—hard words, long words, irregular words and abstract words—but he knows that readers thirst for simple, concrete and familiar words. He conveys complex ideas with plain and simple words. He never delivers his message in a fog of jargon.

Persuasive prose is calculated. A persuasive writer cares about communication and seizes control of his literary fate—guiding the writing process from start to finish. He knows why he writes, what he writes and how he writes. He anticipates, remembers and meets the preferences and expectations of his readers. He knows the power of blank space and the benefits of priming.

Persuasive prose is peppered with concrete words and images. A persuasive writer recognizes that communication comes first. He knows that abstractions extract a toll on the reader's brain, so he chooses the path of clarity and comprehension. He does not embrace an abstract style because it's been used. He knows that advocates have clung to abstract grammar and abstract words for hundreds of years, but he forsakes obtuse writing (even at the risk of offending musty conformists) because it harms the cause of communication.

Persuasive prose plucks the meaningful from the meaningless. A persuasive writer understands the nuances of his argument, its strengths and weaknesses, and he uses that knowledge to disentangle the issues and unscramble the facts.

Persuasive prose is grounded in the writer's personal experience. A persuasive writer knows what has worked in the past, knows what moves him and leverages that experience to improve. He reads persuasive prose and reverse-engineers its language, style and approach.

Persuasive prose accepts nothing less than total comprehension. A persuasive writer knows how his document fits together—from sentence to sentence, paragraph to paragraph.

And last, persuasive prose is the end product of several drafts and hard decisions. A persuasive writer discards any stubborn, unproductive attachment to his own words and thoughts. He brings fresh eyes to the task and makes lucid decisions. As one Tibetan monk said: "In cultivating the fruit tree of good storytelling, never let the foliage obscure the fruit."

ACKNOWLEDGMENTS

This book was made possible by the wisdom and hard work of colleagues and clerks. A big thank you to Judge Barry Silverman, Judge Michael Ambri, Justice Clint Bolick, Justice John Lopez, Judge Cynthia Bailey, Judge Jennifer Perkins, Vanessa Kubota, Iris Lim, Nick Hodder, Brad Greenberger and Ashley Lin.

I also want to thank the folks who read and improved the manuscript: Steven Pinker, Gene Volokh, Brahm Resnick, Barak Orbach, Steve Twist, Marion Weinzweig, Eric Martínez and Connie Mableson, my literary attorney. I want to thank Bryan Kay and Lorraine Murray at the American Bar Association, and my editor, Molly Montanaro, for her hard work and helpful advice.

And my partner in crime, Lauren Weinzweig. Without her, there would be no book.

APPENDIX I

Transition Cheat Sheet

To add a point
Above that
Additionally
Along with
Alongside that
Also
And
Another reason
Apart from that
As well as
Besides
Beyond that
Even more
For their part
Further
Furthermore
In addition
Moreover
Nor
On top of
To this, add that
Together with
What is more

To conclude
Accordingly
After all
All in all
All things considered
Altogether
As is apparent
As noted
As shown
At bottom
By and large
Consequently
Finally
Hence
In brief
In conclusion
In either case
In short
In sum
In the end
In the long run
Last, lastly
On balance
On the whole
Taken together
Then
Therefore
Thus
To sum up
To summarize

To clarify
Actually
Especially
For example
In other words
In short
Particularly
Put simply
Stated differently
To illustrate

To compare/ draw analogy

As in X, Y
As with X, Y
By analogy
By extension
By the same token
Here
In each case
In like manner
In similar fashion
In the same way
Just as X, so Y
Like X, Y
Likewise
Similarly
So too here
So too with

To concede

Admittedly
All the same
Although
At least
At most
At the same time
But
Despite
Even assuming
Even if
Even so
Even still
Even though
Even under
For all that
However
Nevertheless
Of course
On the other hand
Otherwise
Regardless
Still
That may be true, but
That said
Though some argue
To be sure
True enough

To contrast

After all
Alternatively
Although
And yet
At the same time
But
By contrast
Despite
For all that
However
In contrast
Instead
Nevertheless
Not
On one hand
On the contrary
On the other hand
Otherwise
Rather
Unlike (in/this/that)
Yet

To emphasize or expand

Above all
All the more because
All the more reason
All the more X since Y
By extension
Especially
Even more
If anything
In effect
In fact
In other words
In particular
Indeed
More important[ly]
Most important[ly]
Not only X, but Y
Particularly
Put another way
Put differently
Simply put
To repeat

To extract/ stress essence

At bottom
At its core
At its root
At minimum
In effect
In essence
In the end
More to the point
The bottom line is

To give an example

As an example
As in
By way of example
Consider
First, second, third
For example
For instance
For one thing
In that regard
Including
Just imagine
Like
Say
Such as
Suppose
Take
That is
To demonstrate
To illustrate

To list

Additionally
Again
Also
Besides
Even more
Finally
First, second, third
Further
Furthermore
Last
Lastly
Moreover
Next
So too
To begin
To start

To say purpose

For this purpose
In order that
So that
To that end
To this end

To show cause and effect

And so
And therefore
And thus
As a result
Because
Consequently
For
For that reason
On account of
On that basis
Since
So
That is why
Therefore
Thus
To that end
To this end
With that in mind

To redirect

At any rate
From there
Moving on
Turning to

Space, place, location

Above
Across
Adjacent to
Against that backdrop
Against this backdrop
Along
Alongside
Amid
Among
Around
Before

Behind
Below
Beneath
Beside
Between
Beyond
Down
Everywhere
From
Further
Here
Here and there
In front of
In the background
In the center
In the distance
In the foreground
In the middle
Near
Nearby
Next
On this/that side
Opposite to
Over
Parallel with
There
To the left/right
Under
Up
Where

TIME AND SEQUENCE

A moment later
A week earlier
A week later
About
After
Afterward
All of a sudden
All the while
As long as
As soon as
At present
At the present time
At the same time
At this instance
Before
Beforehand
Earlier
Finally
First, second, third
From time to time
Immediately
In due time
In the first place
In the meantime
Last
Later
Never
Next
Now
Once
Out of nowhere
Quickly
Since
Since then
Six months later
So far
Soon
Sooner or later
Subsequently
The next day
The next month
Then
This time
Till
To begin with
Until
Until now
When
Without delay

APPENDIX II

One Word Is Often Enough

Bloated	Lean
as a result of	because, so
as an initial matter	first
at a later date	later
at odds with	conflict
at such place as	where
at such time as	when
at that point in time	then
at the present time	now
at this juncture	now
aware of	know
be subjected to	face
brought about the organization of	organized
by means of	by
by reason of	because

Bloated	Lean
conducts a review of	reviews
dating back to	from
despite the fact that	although
did not hear any	heard no
does not contain	lacks, omits
duly notify	notify
each and every	all
entered into an agreement	agreed
filed a lawsuit	sued
filed a motion	moved
for the purpose of	to
for the reason that	because
has power to	may
in a timely manner	timely, promptly
in addition to	and
in favor of	for
in lieu of	instead
in order that	so
in order to	to
in respect of	about
in the event that	if
in the future	later

Bloated	Lean
in the matter of	about
in the vicinity of	near
in view of the fact that	since
informed of	told
is able to	can
is binding upon	binds
is capable of	can
is dedicated to providing	provides
is in direct conflict	conflicts
is not required to	need not
is of interest to	interests
is unable to	cannot
it is imperative that we	we must
made the decision	decided
make an appearance	appear
mutually agree	agree
offers testimony	testifies
on a daily basis	daily
on the basis that	because
owing to the fact that	because
performed a search of	searched
prior to	before

Bloated	Lean
provided information	explained
pursuant to	under
referred to as	called
regardless of	no matter
relating to the subject of	about, regarding
sufficient number of	enough
taken into account	considered
to the extent that	if
was in violation of	violated
went on to	then, later
were in great need of	needed
with respect to	about
without delay	now

APPENDIX III

Answers to Questions

Chap. 3, § 4(D). Revise this sentence without nominalizations.

1. Despite all the efforts of Zen experts, however, the insight afforded to us Europeans into the essence of Zen has remained exceedingly scanty; as though it resisted deeper penetration, after a few steps one's groping intuition comes up against insurmountable barriers. (41)
   Europeans have not learned much about Zen and have been unable to teach themselves. (14)[1]

Chap. 3, § 4(G). Revise these sentences without nominalizations.

1. The contract clearly contained numerous components.[2]
   The contract had many parts.

[1] The first sentence contains three nominalizations formed from verbs and adjectives, and it never tells us who is doing what. The sentence springs to life when we eliminate or reanimate the zombie nouns and add the human actor. Zero nominalizations remain.

[2] Badverb, abstract verbs, nouns and adjectives.

2. Louisiana law makes a distinction between general and specific guarantees.[3]
Louisiana law distinguishes between general and specific guarantees.

3. He offered testimony about his residence, inter alia, after the trial commenced.[4]
He testified about his home and more at trial.

4. There are statutory prohibitions against obviously absurd unreasonable actions.[5]
Unreasonable actions are prohibited by statute.

5. He made a decision to proceed ex post facto for the attainment of justice.[6]
He decided to achieve justice retroactively.

6. In view of the fact that the defendant never made an appearance, the court terminated the remainder of trial.
The court ended trial because the defendant never appeared.

---

[3] Nominalization.
[4] Nominalization, Latin, long word.
[5] Badverb, nominalization and redundant.
[6] Latin, two nominalizations.

7. Johnson is desirous of making the ultimate utilization of the real property to obtain the maximum income and return from this most valuable and unique parcel of real property containing a massive sand and gravel deposit. (36)
   Johnson wants to maximize the value of the sand and gravel deposits. (12)

8. After the expiration of the time, our team scored a touchdown.
   Our team scored a touchdown after time expired.

9. If the question had been raised below, the situation might have been met ipso facto by way of additional proof.[7]
   Plaintiff might have offered more proof had the defendant raised the issue in the trial court.

10. Plaintiff took transportation from Paris to London when he was arrested.
    Plaintiff traveled from Paris to London where he was arrested.

---

[7] This sentence is teeming with passive verb construction (had been, have met), laden with prepositions (by way of) and abstract nouns (question, situation, additional), and sprinkled with jargon (ipso facto), all of which result in the near erasure of human agency.

11. While Jones was affiliated with the Phoenix Police Department as an investigator, he was a chaplain for two months in 2025, where he conducted Sunday Mass.
    When Jones was a Phoenix police investigator, he also served as a chaplain at Sunday Mass for two months in 2025.

12. The erroneous statements of fact in the trial court's ruling necessitates reversal of the trial court's decision.
    The trial court must be reversed because it got the facts wrong.

Chap. 3, § 7. Rewrite sentences to fix sentence structure. Focus on structure, not word choice or concision.

1. After returning from her honeymoon in New Orleans, the business conference in St. Lucia, and a visit to her parents in Paris, she was fired.[8]
   She was fired after returning from her honeymoon in New Orleans, the business trip to St. Lucia and a visit to her parents in Paris.

2. Louisiana is obliged, pursuant to the opinion and consent decree issued by the federal district court in *Cane v. Able*, 24 F.Supp.2d 209

[8] Use subject and verb in first seven letters. Eliminate center-embedded clause.

(D. La. 2022), to expedite its development of standards.[9]
Louisiana must accelerate its development of standards under federal law. See Cane v. Able, 24 F.Supp.2d 209 (D. La. 2022).

3. Bob appealed for special action relief, reversing the entry of summary judgment on his claims for tortious interference with contractual relations and breach of the implied covenant of good faith and fair dealing, to the court of appeals.[10]
Bob appealed to the court of appeals for special action relief to reverse the entry of summary judgment on his claims for tortious interference with contractual relations and breach of the implied covenant of good faith and fair dealing.

4. After a nine-day trial, during which the superior court precluded reference to the Sedona incident, the jury found Tucker guilty of second-degree murder.[11]
The jury found Tucker guilty of second-degree murder after a nine-day trial in which the superior court precluded reference to the Sedona incident.

[9] Keep noun and verb together.
[10] Eliminate center-embedded clause.
[11] Use subject and verb in first seven letters. Eliminate center-embedded clause.

5. Police in the States of Arizona, Georgia, and Louisiana must confiscate all drug paraphernalia.[12]
Police must confiscate all drug paraphernalia in the States of Arizona, Georgia, and Louisiana.

6. In the first case, which involved an oral contract for an indefinite period of time under which a distributor exclusively distributed a product though a 21-county area in which the product had not been previously sold, the court agreed it was legal.[13]
The court upheld an oral exclusive distribution contract in the first case. That contract indefinitely granted a distributor exclusive rights to sell a product in 21 counties where it had never been sold before.

7. His argument that defendant failed to provide a verbal warning about the spikes that caused his injury fails because he knew of the hazard and failed to conduct himself accordingly.[14]

---

[12] Keep noun and verb together.
[13] Use subject and noun in first seven letters. Eliminate center-embedded clause.
[14] Keep noun and verb together; use subject and verb in first seven letters.

He argued defendant failed to verbally warn him about the spikes that caused his injury, but that argument fails because he knew about the hazard and took no precautions.

8. There is no time restriction for challenging a void judgment.
   A void judgment may be challenged at any time.

Turn passive voice into active voice.

1. The letter was written in error.
   He/she wrote the letter in error.

2. It is expected that the hearing will end soon.
   We expect the hearing to end soon.

3. Another justice was appointed by the Governor.
   The Governor appointed another justice.

4. There was no discussion about the deal at the holiday party.
   They did not discuss the deal at the holiday party.

Identify the passive voice (circle) and nominalizations (underline).

> A regard for style should ultimately be motivated by a desire for effective communication,

which is essential to all human interaction. Understanding of this idea may be better instilled in students through the instruction of style in a flexible manner. This may be accomplished by presenting style as a guide to writing (perhaps applied only after a piece has been written) rather than a restriction placed upon writing.

A **regard** for style should ultimately be motivated by a **desire** for effective **communication**, which is essential to all human **interaction**. **Understanding** of this idea may be better instilled in students through the **instruction** of style in a flexible manner. This may be accomplished by presenting style as a **guide** to writing (perhaps applied only after a piece has been written) rather than a **restriction** placed upon **writing**.

This paragraph has nine zombie nouns and seven agentless passives.

Chap. 3, § 8. Read these quotes and identify each as a metaphor or simile.

Metaphor

Simile

Metaphor

Chap. 4, § 5. Identify meaningful words and adhesive words; then rewrite to decrease word count.

1. There is no evidence to support Plaintiff's contention.
   No evidence supports Plaintiff's claim.

2. The motion filed by the defendant was meritless for the reason that it ignored the events prior to the accident.

   The motion filed by the defendant was meritless for the reason that it ignored the events prior to the accident.

   The defendant's motion was meritless because it ignored the events before the accident.

Rewrite sentences to omit needless words.

1. Based on prior experience, it is imperative that we secure a sufficient number of class representatives.
   We must secure enough class representatives.

2. Despite the fact that he performed a search, the child was never found.
   He searched but never found the child.

3. The contractual agreement provides that costs will be reimbursed up to a maximum of $1,000 dollars a month.
   The contract caps monthly reimbursements at $1,000.

4. In the event that he makes a decision on whether to leave the corporation, management must be told.
   Management must be told if he decides to quit.

5. There are two reasons the *Bonds* case is distinguishable.
   Bonds is distinguishable for two reasons.

6. The simple truth is that plaintiff dropped the ball and failed to comply with the clear and straightforward requirements of the Act.
   Plaintiff failed to satisfy the Act.

7. I hope and desire for peace and quiet on all days, save and except for my birthday.
   I hope for quiet on all days but my birthday.

8. It is axiomatic that he breached the contract.
   He breached the contract.

9. He walked a distance of 12 miles before the roads merged together.
   He walked 12 miles before the roads merged.

10. A loud but incoherent murmur arose from the crowd that had gathered.
    A loud but incoherent murmur arose from the crowd.

Reduce the number of words in this paragraph without losing the point:

1. The Arizona Supreme Court adopted substantial changes to Rule 609 in the year 2012. Previously Rule 609 did not distinguish between civil and criminal cases; it applied equally to all cases. Nor did the previous version of the rule distinguish between defendants and non-defendants; it applied to all witnesses regardless of whether he or she was a party to the case. By adopting the distinctions between civil and criminal cases and between the status of a non-party, the Supreme Court indicated that impeaching non-defendant with all the particulars of his or her prior conviction is required without any weighing of the mere probative value versus prejudice. Therefore, the particulars for which the testifying non-defendant witness had been convicted should have been admitted for the jury's consideration in assessing his credibility. (130)
The defense should have been allowed to impeach all witnesses based on their prior convictions. The Arizona Supreme Court changed Rule 609 in 2012 to distinguish between civil and criminal cases, recognizing that witnesses in criminal trials may be impeached by a prior conviction without regard to the testimony's probative value or prejudice. (53)

Chap. 5, § 2. Read the short narrative text below. Mark the tools of cohesion: italicize transitions, underline parallel construction and bold pronouns.

1. **We** wanted to swim, *but* the pool was dirty with fungus growing on its walls. **That** was unnerving to **our** mother, who didn't want **us** to get sick. *If* **we** got sick, **we'd** need to miss school and that was not an option. *As a result*, we did not swim.

2. Moe ran the red light and plowed into the pedestrian. The pedestrian was thrown from the street onto the sidewalk. Random motorists pulled over to help the pedestrian. *In contrast*, Moe left the scene. *Afterward*, a fire truck arrived with a medic. **That** medic tried to revive the pedestrian, but could not.

Add the transitional word or phrase wherever you think it fits best to show how one sentence relates to another. Which transitions?

1. Bob is a vegetarian, __ Todd eats meat.
   Bob is a vegetarian, but Todd eats meat.

2. Phoenix is sunny in the summer. _____, San Diego and Los Angeles are sunny.
   Phoenix is sunny in the summer. Likewise, San Diego and Los Angeles are sunny.

Draft topic sentences for these paragraphs.

1. My mother went to Louisiana State University. My father went to Louisiana Tech University. My sister went to Tulane University.
   My family attended Louisiana universities.

2. San Diego hits 120 degrees in August. Los Angeles hits 115 degrees in July. San Francisco has snow in June.
   The State of California has a wide variety of weather in the summer.

3. The evidence was relevant to the issue. It caused little prejudice. At the same time, it had great probative value. It was not hearsay. And the jury received a curative instruction.
   Plaintiffs have shown no error. The evidence was admissible.

The sentences of this paragraph are out of order. Fix that.

1. (3) At two months old, Child was rushed to the hospital with life-threatening brain injuries. (2) Mother and Father are the biological parents of Child, who was born healthy in Nevada in 2011. (4) Father was later convicted in Nevada of abusing his daughter and sentenced to prison. (5) Child suffered severe and irreversible brain damage. (6) She now endures many chronic and debilitating disorders, including encephalopathy, spastic quadriplegic cerebral palsy and epilepsy. (7) She requires a wheelchair and is legally blind; cannot feed herself or communicate; and bears a perpetual high risk for seizures. (8) Child needs full-time care to survive. (1) This is a child dependency action.
   This is a child dependency action. Mother and Father are the biological parents of Child, who was born healthy in Nevada in 2011. At two months old, Child was rushed to the hospital with life-threatening brain injuries. Father was later convicted in Nevada of abusing his daughter and sentenced to prison. Child suffered severe and irreversible brain damage. She now endures many chronic and debilitating disorders, including encephalopathy, spastic quadriplegic cerebral palsy and epilepsy.

She requires a wheelchair and is legally blind; cannot feed herself or communicate; and bears a perpetual high risk for seizures. Child needs full-time care to survive.

Chap. 9, § 5. Rewrite for clarity and concision.

1. For the purpose of orderly administration and the attainment of justice, certain rules are established. Any rule the enforcement of which results in a failure of justice should be carefully scrutinized and not blindly adhered to unless the abandonment of it will work more injustice than will follow if it be adhered to. (53)
   Courts adopt rules to promote justice, but these rules are not absolute and should be abandoned when they cause more injustice than they avoid. (24)

2. I have tried to keep my language as simple as possible. Not only because Zen teaches and advocates the greatest economy of expression and because I have found that what I cannot say quite simply and without recourse to mystic jargon has not become sufficiently clear and concrete even to myself. (51)
   I have used simple words because Zen says to say more with less, and because it helps me understand. (19)

3. In numerous cases over numerous decades, this Court has acknowledged that the First Amendment is applicable in situations in which the government, acting not as sovereign but as employer, places limits upon its workers' speech. (35)

   This court has long recognized that government employees have First Amendment rights. (12)

4. The Seventh Circuit has indicated that any doubts concerning the arbitrability of claims should be resolved in favor of arbitration. *Rodgers v. Central Hospital*, 783 F.2d 485 (7th Cir. 1993). In *Rodgers*, the court stated: "The Arbitration Act establishes that as a matter of law any doubts concerning the scope of arbitrable issues and whether a claim should be arbitrated should be resolved in favor of arbitration." (67)

   The Seventh Circuit resolves doubts of arbitrability in favor of arbitration. (11)

ENDNOTES

[1] Stephen King, On Writing: A Memoir of the Craft (Pocket Books 2000).
[2] Eugen Herrigel, Zen in the Art of Archery (Routledge & Kegan Paul 1953).
[3] Bryan A. Garner, *Interviews with United States Supreme Court Justices: Ruth Bader Ginsburg*, 13 Scribes J. of Legal Writing 134 (2010).
[4] Thomas Paine, Common Sense (1776).
[5] This quote is often attributed to the Irish playwright George Bernard Shaw, but some people doubt he ever said it. Alan Alda, If I Understood You, Would I Have This Look on My Face? xi (Random House 2017).
[6] 3 Collected Works of Abraham Lincoln (Aug. 21, 1858–Mar. 4, 1860) (digital collection).
[7] Antonin Scalia, Scalia Speaks 60 (Crown Forum 2017).
[8] Aristotle, Rhetoric, bk. I, ch. 3.
[9] E. Fedorenko & R. Varley, *Language and Thought Are Not the Same Thing: Evidence from Neuroimaging and Neurological Patients*, 1369(1) Ann. N. Y. Acad. Sci. 132–53 (Apr. 2016).
[10] Yellowlees Douglas, The Reader's Brain 20 (Cambridge Univ. Press) (2015).
[11] Anne Janzen, Writing to Be Understood: What Works and Why 94 (Cuesta Park Consulting 2018).
[12] Douglas, *supra* note 10.
[13] W.C. West & P.J. Holcomb, *Imaginal, Semantic, and Surface-Level Processing of Concrete and Abstract Words: An Electrophysiological Investigation*, 12(6) J. Cog. Neurosci. 1024–37 (2000).
[14] Tom Albrighton, How to Write Clearly, ch. 1 (ABC Bus. Commc'ns Ltd. 2021).
[15] Bruce W. A. Whittlesea, Larry L. Jacoby & Krista Girard, *Illusions of Immediate Memory: Evidence of an Attributional*

Basis for Feelings of Familiarity and Perceptual Quality, 29 J. Memory & Lang. 716 (1990).
[16] James W. McElhany, Legal Writing That Works, 93 ABA J. (July 1, 2007).
[17] The Simpsons: *How I Spent My Strummer Vacation* (Fox television broadcast, Nov. 10, 2002).
[18] R.N.S. Topping, The Elements of Rhetoric, How to Write and Speak Clearly & Persuasively (Angelico Press 2016).
[19] Irin Carmon & Shana Knizhnik, Notorious RBG 121 (Dey St. Books 2015).
[20] *Id.*
[21] Daniel Webster (1849).
[22] West & Holcomb, *supra* note 13, at 1024.
[23] *Id.*
[24] Sandy F. Kraemer, Will Rogers—the Legal Profession's Best Critic, 59 ABA J. 1431 (Dec. 1973).
[25] Victor Feraru, *Jargon, Legalese and the Bluebook: My Conversation With Judge Richard A. Posner*, Huffington Post (Dec. 30, 2016).
[26] George Orwell, Politics and the English Language (Penguin 2013).
[27] Arnold Samuelson, With Hemingway: A Year in Key West and Cuba 11 (Random House 1984).
[28] F. Reed Dickerson, Clear Legal Drafting: What's Holding Us Back? 150 (1980).
[29] Eric Martínez, Francis Mollica & Edward Gibson, *Even Laypeople Use Legalese*, Proc. Nat'l Acad. Sci. U.S.A. 121 (2024).
[30] Joseph M. Williams, Style: Lessons in Clarity and Grace 6 (Pearson Educ., Inc. 2014).
[31] Aristotle, Aristotle's Nicomachean Ethics (R.C. Bartlett & S.D. Collins eds., Univ. of Chi. Press 2011).
[32] Thomas Jefferson, Autobiography ch. 4, doc. 7 (1821).
[33] Learned Hand, *Is There a Common Will*, 28 Mich. L. Rev. 46, 52 (1929).
[34] Shawn Burton, *The Case for Plain-Language Contracts* (Jan.–Feb. 2018).

[35] *Id.*
[36] *Id.*
[37] *Id.*
[38] *Id.*
[39] Mark Twain letter (Oct. 15, 1888).
[40] Harvard Health Publishing, *Doctor-Patient Communication: A Shared Responsibility* (Aug. 1, 2007).
[41] ARISTOTLE, ARISTOTLE'S POETICS (Hill & Wang 1961).
[42] *Eric Martínez*, MASS. INST. OF TECH., https://saxelab.mit.edu/lab_members/eric-martinez (last visited Nov. 17, 2024).
[43] *Id.*
[44] Daniel Oppenheimer, *Consequences of Erudite Vernacular Utilized Irrespective of Necessity: Problems with Using Long Words Needlessly*, 20 APPLIED COGNITIVE PSYCH. 139, 140–47 (2006).
[45] *Id.*
[46] Warren L. Nooshin, Matthew Farmer, Tianyu Gu & Caleb Warren, *Marketing Ideas: How to Write Research Articles That Readers Understand and Cite*, 85 J. MKTG. 42 (2021).
[47] ORWELL, *supra* note 26.
[48] BILL BRYSON, MOTHER TONGUE (Penguin Books 2009).
[49] James W. Pennebaker & Thomas C. Lay, *Language Use and Personality During Crises: Analyses of Mayor Rudolph Giuliani's Press Conferences*, 36 J. RSCH. IN PERSONALITY 271, 279–81 (2002).
[50] Oppenheimer, *supra* note 44, at 153 (citing Pennebaker & Lay, *supra* note 49, at 271).
[51] Oppenheimer, *supra* note 44, at 153.
[52] Pennebaker & Lay, *supra* note 49, at 279–81.
[53] Eric Martínez, Francis Mollica & Edward Gibson, *Poor Writing, Not Specialized Concepts, Drives Processing Difficulty in Legal Language*, 224 COGNITION 1, 6 (2022).
[54] *Id.*
[55] Eric Martínez, Francis Mollica & Edward Gibson, *Even Lawyers Do Not Like Legalese*, 120 PNAS 1, 3 (2023).
[56] Albert Einstein lecture (1931).
[57] CARMON & KNIZHNIK, *supra* note 19.

[58] ANNE JANZEN, WRITING TO BE UNDERSTOOD: WHAT WORKS AND WHY 95 (Cuesta Park Consulting 2018).

[59] Amicus Curiae Brief at 4–5, Novak v. City of Parma, 33 F.4th 296 (6th Cir. 2022).

[60] Steven Clifton, Lyn Frazier & Cynthia Connine, *Lexical Expectations in Sentence Comprehension*, 23(6) J. VERBAL LEARNING & VERBAL BEHAVIOR 696–708 (1984).

[61] Alexandra Klepp, Vanessa Niccolai, Giovanni Buccino & Alfons Schnitzler, *Action Verb Processing Specifically Modulates Motor Behaviour and Sensorimotor Neuronal Oscillations*, 9 SCI. REPS. (2019); Vanessa Niccolai, Alexandra Klepp & Alfons Schnitzler, *Brain Signatures of Embodied Semantics and Language: A Consensus Paper*, 6(1) J. COGNITION (2023).

[62] Hon. Robert Jackson, *Advocacy Before the United States Supreme Court*, 37 CORNELL L.Q. 1 (1951).

[63] BRYAN A. GARNER, GARNER ON LANGUAGE AND WRITING (ABA 2009).

[64] MICHEL THOMAS, SPEAK GERMAN WITH MICHEL THOMAS, Disc 5 (McGraw Hill 2001).

[65] Friederici Fiebach, *Processing Concrete Words: fMRI Evidence Against a Specific Right-Hemisphere Involvement*, 42 NEUROPSYCHOLOGIA 62 (2004).

[66] STEVEN PINKER, THE SENSE OF STYLE: THE THINKING PERSON'S GUIDE TO WRITING IN THE 21ST CENTURY 72 (2014).

[67] ARISTOTLE, TOPICS 108a.

[68] Paul Hoffman & Matthew Bair, *How Do Brain Regions Specialised for Concrete and Abstract Concepts Align with Functional Brain Networks? A Neuroimaging Meta-Analysis*, NEUROSCI. & BIOBEHAV. REVS. 174 (2025).

[69] Robert P. Charrow & Veda R. Charrow, *Making Legal Language Understandable: A Psycholinguistic Analysis of Jury Instructions*, 79 COLUM. L. REV. 1306, 1321 (1979) ("Anything that makes a verb less verb-like and more noun-like creates abstraction.").

[70] PINKER, *supra* note 66, at 52.

[71] E.B. Coleman, *The Comprehensibility of Several Grammatical Transformations*, 48 J. APPLIED PSYCH. 186, 186 (1964)

(showing nominalizations are slower to read); Iria Bello, *Cognitive Implications of Nominalizations in the Advancement of Scientific Discourse*, INT'L J. ENG. STUDIES 19 (Aug. 2016).

[72] Lloyd R. Bostian, *Dysfunctional Pseudo-Elegance: Why Passive and Nominal Writing Fails*, 65 J. APPLIED COMMC'NS 32, 38 (1982); E.B. Coleman, *Learning of Prose Written in Four Grammatical Transformations*, 49 J. APPLIED PSYCH. 332, 336 ("Actives were better retained than passives for all scoring systems."); Coleman, *supra* note 71, at 188 (showing nominalizations made it harder for readers to recall the content of the sentences).

[73] Coleman, *supra* note 72 ("Actives were better retained than passives for all scoring systems."); Coleman, *supra* note 71 (showing it is hard for readers to remember content in sentences with nominalizations); I. Bello, *Cognitive Implications of Nominalizations in the Advancement of Scientific Discourse*, INT'L J. ENG. STUDIES (Aug. 2016).

[74] Steven Pinker, *Legal Writing Meets Cognitive Linguistics*, Sandra Day O'Connor College of Law, Arizona State University (Oct. 5, 2023).

[75] *Id.*

[76] Trump v. United States, 603 U.S. 593, 639 (2024).

[77] *Id.*

[78] Coleman, *supra* note 71, at 190.

[79] HERRIGEL, *supra* note 2.

[80] *Id.*

[81] KING, *supra* note 1.

[82] EDWARD ST. AUBYN, PATRICK MELROSE: BAD NEWS (Picador USA).

[83] Lance N. Long & William F. Christensen, *Clearly, Using Intensifiers Is Very Bad—Or Is It?*, 45 IDAHO L. REV. 171, 171 (2008).

[84] BENJAMIN N. CARDOZO, LAW AND LITERATURE (Harcourt Brace 1931).

[85] Andrew Ross Sorkin, *One of the Most Hated People in the World*, N.Y. TIMES (Sept. 16, 2023).

[86] Kate Kiefer Lee, *Mark Twain On Writing*, FORBES (Nov. 30, 2020).
[87] MARK DAWIDZIAK, MARK MY WORDS: MARK TWAIN ON WRITING (St. Martin's Press 1996).
[88] www.etymonline.com/word/however (last visited Oct. 1, 2024).
[89] JOAN DIDION, LET ME TELL YOU WHAT I MEAN (Knopf Doubleday 2022).
[90] LEWIS CARROLL, POETA FIT, NON NASCITUR (1869).
[91] ERNEST HEMINGWAY, DEATH IN THE AFTERNOON (Charles Scribner's Sons Publication 1932).
[92] JOHN HERSEY, HIROSHIMA (Alfred A. Knopf 1946).
[93] Edward Gibson, *Linguistic Complexity: Locality of Syntactic Dependencies*, 68 COGNITION 1, 1 (1998); Noam Chomsky & George A. Miller, *Introduction to the Formal Analysis of Natural Languages, in* HANDBOOK OF MATH. PSYCH. 2–419 (R. Duncan Luce et al. eds. 1963).
[94] The names of the parties have been changed.
[95] Martínez, Mollica & Gibson, *supra* note 53, at 2.
[96] *Id.* at 6.
[97] JOE MORAN, FIRST YOU WRITE A SENTENCE (Penguin 2019).
[98] The Acropolitan, *Sentence Length Has Declined 75% in the Past 500 Years*, MEDIUM (Aug. 27, 2016), https://medium.com/@theacropolitan/sentence-length-has-declined-75-in-the-past-500-years-2e40f80f589f.
[99] STEPHEN WILBERS, KEYS TO GREAT WRITING (Writer's Digest Books 2000).
[100] It is created by combining the Greek words *para* and *graphos*, which are translated in English to mean *besides* and *in writing*.
[101] Jimmy Stamp, *The Origin of the Pilcrow, aka the Strange Paragraph Symbol*, SMITHSONIAN MAG. (July 10, 2013).
[102] James R. Miller & Walter Kintsch, *Recall and Readability of Short Prose Passages*, 6 J. EXPERIMENTAL PSYCH.: HUMAN LEARNING & MEMORY 335, 351 (1980).
[103] WILLIAM ZINSSER, ON WRITING WELL (Harper Collins 1976).

[104] Bennet B. Murdock, Jr., *The Serial Position Effect of Free Recall*, 64 J. EXPERIMENTAL PSYCH. 482, 487 (1962).
[105] ARISTOTLE, TOPICS 130a; *cf.* TOPICS 139b & 160a.
[106] ARISTOTLE, ACOUSTICS 801b.
[107] Adrian Barnett & Zoe Doubleday, *Meta-Research: The Growth of Acronyms in the Scientific Literature*, ELIFE (2020) (from .4 per 100 words to 4.1 per 100 words).
[108] ORWELL, *supra* note 26.
[109] LEWIS CARROLL, ALICE'S ADVENTURES IN WONDERLAND, ch. 9 (1893).
[110] David Beltrán et al., *Inhibitory Mechanisms in the Processing of Negations: A Neural Reuse Hypothesis*, 50 J. PSYCHOLINGUIST RSCH. 1243 (2021); Carolin Dudschig & Barbara Kaup, *Negation As Conflict: Conflict Adaptation Following Negating Vertical Spatial Words*, 210 BRAIN & LANG. (2020).
[111] Eugene Y. Chan & Sam J. Maglio, *The Voice of Cognition, Active and Passive Voice Influence Distance and Construal*, 46 PERSONALITY & SOC. PSYCH. BULLETIN 547, 555 (2020) (noting a study that found "authors thinking abstractly also tend to use more passive voice constructions in their writing compared with those thinking more concretely").
[112] Bostian, *supra* note 72, at 38 (slower to read, harder to understand, and less interesting); DEBORAH E. BOUCHOUZ, ASPEN HANDBOOK FOR LEGAL WRITERS: A PRACTICAL REFERENCE 87 (2005).
[113] BOUCHOZ, *supra* note 112 ("Readers comprehend a sentence in the active [voice] more quickly because it follows the way they normally process information. They do not have to search through the sentence looking for the actor.").
[114] Fernanda Ferreira, *The Misinterpretation of Noncanonical Sentences*, 47 COGNITIVE PSYCH. 164, 188 (2003); Jennifer E. Mack et al., *Neural Correlates of Processing Passive Sentences*, 3 BRAIN SCIS. 1198, 1202 (2013).
[115] Bostian, *supra* note 72, at 36 (students read the active passages seven percent faster than the passive passages).
[116] Mack et al., *supra* note 115, at 1204.

[117] Coleman, *supra* note 71 (slower reading speed); DANIEL T. WILLINGHAM & CEDAR RIENER, COGNITION: THE THINKING ANIMAL 293 (4th ed. 2019) (harder to process); Coleman, *supra* note 72, at 335 (harder to understand); Lloyd R. Bostian, *How Active, Passive and Nominal Styles Affect Readability of Science Writing*, 60 J.Q. 635, 636 (1983) (slower to read, harder to understand, and less interesting); Mack et al., *supra* note 115, at 1200 (longer reaction times for passive sentence).
[118] BRYAN A. GARNER, GARNER'S MODERN AMERICAN USAGE 613 (2009).
[119] Martínez, Mollica & Gibson, *supra* note 53, at 5.
[120] *Id.* at 2 (citing Brian J. Baldie, *The Acquisition of the Passive Voice*, J. CHILD LANG. 331–48 (1976)).
[121] Daniel Skinner & Steven Pludwin, *Unsought Responsibility: The U.S. Supreme Court and the Politics of Passive Writing*, 45 POLITY 499, 513, 521 (2013).
[122] A defense attorney might use passive voice to focus or deflect the court from good or bad facts or to create distance between their client and a crime. A prosecutor might use active voice to make the reader feel closer to the action.
[123] Skinner & Pludwin, *supra* note 121.
[124] Eugene Chan & Sam Maglio, *The Voice of Cognition, Active and Passive Voice Influence Distance and Construal*, 46 PERSONALITY & SOC. PSYCH. BULL. 547, 549–50, 555 (2020).
[125] WILLIAM STRUNK & E.B. WHITE, THE ELEMENTS OF STYLE 18 (4th ed. 2000).
[126] *Id.*
[127] Pinker, *supra* note 74.
[128] James Fallows, *The Networks Blew the Call*, THE ATLANTIC (Jan. 8, 2019).
[129] ALLAN PAIVIO, IMAGERY AND VERBAL PROCESSES (Holt, Rinehart & Winston 1971); ALLAN PAIVIO, MENTAL REPRESENTATIONS (Oxford Univ. Press 1986).
[130] Simon Lacey, et al., *Metaphorically Feeling: Comprehending Textural Metaphors Activates Somatosensory Cortex*, 120(3) BRAIN LANG. 416–21 (2012).

[131] Emory News Center, *Hearing Metaphors Activates Sensory Brain Regions* (Feb. 6, 2012).
[132] ARISTOTLE, ARISTOTLE'S POETICS (Hill & Wang 1961).
[133] Letter to Cassandra Austen (Jan. 24, 1809).
[134] *See* Defendant's Amicus Response to Plaintiffs' Motion for Preliminary Injunction, Ariz. Citizens Clean Elections Com'n, et al. v. Bennett, CV2013-010338 (Maricopa Super. Ct.).
[135] *See* Response to Motion for Temporary Restraining Order, Hasbro v. Four Star Int'l Trading Co., Kenneth Plevan, Skadden Arps.
[136] Reynolds v. Sims, 377 U.S. 533, 562 (1964).
[137] Smith v. Arizona, 602 U.S. __ (2024).
[138] Pinker, *supra* note 74.
[139] TRACY KIDDER, GOOD PROSE: THE ART OF NONFICTION (Penguin 2013).
[140] PAIVIO, IMAGERY, *supra* note 129.
[141] ALLAN PAIVIO, DUAL CODING THEORY IN MENTAL REPRESENTATIONS: A DUAL CODING APPROACH 583–605 (Oxford Univ. Press 1990).
[142] ARISTOTLE, DE ANIMA (ON THE SOUL), bk. 3, ch. 7.
[143] Richard A. Posner, *Legal Writing Today*, 8 SCRIBES J. LEGAL WRITING 36 (2001-2002).
[144] JOHN GREGORY DUNNE, CROONING 196 (Random House 1994).
[145] FORREST GUMP (Paramount Pictures 1994).
[146] William Faulkner, Speech, Univ. of Miss. (Apr. 1949).
[147] https://quoteinvestigator.com/2016/01/26/dictionary/ (last visited Nov. 3, 2024).
[148] ERNEST HEMINGWAY, FOR WHOM THE BELL TOLLS (Scribner 1940).
[149] WILLIAM FAULKNER, THE SOUND AND THE FURY (Random House corr. ed. 1984).
[150] GEORGE ORWELL, DOWN AND OUT IN PARIS AND LONDON (Harcourt, Brace 1950).

[151] Bryan A. Garner, *Interviews with United States Supreme Court Justices*, 13 SCRIBES J. LEGAL WRITING 35 (2010).
[152] Irin Carmon, *The Glorious RBG*, INTELLIGENCER, N.Y. MAG. (Sep. 18, 2020).
[153] Leonore Fleischer, *Talk of the Trade*, 227 PUBLISHERS WEEKLY 10 (Mar. 8, 1985).
[154] RAY BRADBURY, ZEN IN THE ART OF WRITING 145 (Joshua Odell Editions 1989).
[155] SUN TZU, THE ART OF WAR, ch. 6 (Capstone Publ'g 2010).
[156] WILLIAM SHAKESPEARE, HAMLET, act 2, sc. 2 (Oxford Univ. Press 2008).
[157] Benjamin N. Cardozo, *Law and Literature*, 39 COLUM. L. REV. 119, 126, 52 HARV. L. REV. 471, 478, 48 YALE L.J. 489, 496 (1939) (simultaneously published).
[158] Jackson, *supra* note 62.
[159] STEPHEN BUDIANSKY, OLIVER WENDELL HOLMES: A LIFE IN WAR, LAW, AND IDEAS (W. W. Norton & Co. 2019).
[160] WINSTON CHURCHILL, CHURCHILL BY HIMSELF 50 (Public Affairs 2008).
[161] JOHN LOCKE, AN ESSAY CONCERNING HUMAN UNDERSTANDING (1690).
[162] Letter to law student John Minor (Aug. 30, 1814).
[163] RICHARD C. WYDICK, PLAIN ENGLISH FOR LAWYERS (Carolina Acad. Press, 5th ed. 2005).
[164] C.J. Liu & S.M. Rawl, *Effects of Text Cohesion on Comprehension and Retention of Colorectal Cancer Screening Information: A Preliminary Study*, J. HEALTH COMMC'N 222–40 (2012) ("Higher text cohesion showed a significant effect on reading times and text comprehension but not on word recognition and recall."); M. GERNSBACHER, LANGUAGE COMPREHENSION AS STRUCTURE BUILDING (1990).
[165] JOSEPH M. WILLIAMS, STYLE: LESSONS IN CLARITY AND GRACE 178 (Pearson Educ., Inc. 2010).
[166] John McElroy, N. Jacoby & E. Fedorenko, *Discourse-Level Comprehension Engages Medial Frontal Theory of Mind Brain Regions Even For Expository Texts*, 35(6) LANG. COG. NEUROSCI. 780-796 (2020).

[167] ALEXANDER BAIN, ENGLISH COMPOSITION AND RHETORIC (1866 textbook).
[168] https://www.nngroup.com/reports/how-people-read-web-eyetracking-evidence/ (last visited Oct. 8, 2025).
[169] G. Brod, M. Werkle-Bergner & Y.L. Shing, *The Influence of Prior Knowledge on Memory: A Developmental Cognitive Neuroscience Perspective*, FRONT BEHAV. NEUROSCI. (2013).
[170] Liu & Rawl, *supra* note 164.
[171] Julie Lemarié, Robert F. Lorch Jr. & Marie-Paule Péry-Woodley, *Understanding How Headings Influence Text Processing*, 10 DISCOURS 3 (2012) (citing studies).
[172] DANIEL KAHNEMAN, THINKING, FAST AND SLOW 1, 35 (Farrar, Straus and Giroux 2011).
[173] Michael J. Higdon, *Something Judicious This Way Comes . . . the Use of Foreshadowing as a Persuasive Device in Judicial Narrative*, 44 U. RICH. L. REV. 1213, 1225 (2010) ("studies show that when processing messages readers are more persuaded by conclusions that are implicit rather than explicit, especially when the reader is more involved in the communication").
[174] R.B. Zajonc & D.W. Rajecki, *Exposure and Affect: A Field Experiment*, 17 HUM. LEARNING & THINKING 216–17 (1969).
[175] S. Murphy, *Affect, Cognition, and Awareness: Affective Priming With Optimal and Suboptimal Stimulus Exposures*, 64(5) J. PERSONALITY & SOC. PSYCH. 723–39 (1993).
[176] RALPH WALDO EMERSON, GREATNESS, LETTERS AND SOCIAL AIMS 205–218 (James R. Osgood & Co. 1876).
[177] Joe Fassler, *Why Stephen King Spends 'Months and Even Years' Writing Opening Sentences*, THE ATLANTIC (July 23, 2013).
[178] Brief for Appellees, Perry v. Schwarzenegger, 591 F.3d 1147 (9th Cir. 2010) (No. 10-16696) (citation omitted), http://afer.org/wp-content/uploads/2010/10/Brief.pdf.
[179] Brief of Counterclaim Defendant-Appellee Hartford Fire Insurance Company, World Trade Ctr. Properties, L.L.C. v. Hartford Fire Ins. Co., 345 F.3d 154 (2d Cir. 2003).
[180] Linda Kuehl, *Joan Didion, The Art of Fiction*, 71 PARIS REV. (Fall–Winter 1978).

[181] L. Nadel & K.C. Simon, *Perceived Memory Credibility: The Role of Details*, 121(52) PROC. NAT'L ACAD. SCI. U.S.A. (2024).
[182] BENJAMIN CARDOZO, LAW AND LITERATURE (Harcourt 1925).
[183] *Id.*
[184] ANTONIN SCALIA & BRYAN GARNER, MAKING YOUR CASE: THE ART OF PERSUADING JUDGES 94 (2008).
[185] RICHARD A. POSNER, REFLECTIONS ON JUDGING 276–277 (Harvard Univ. Press 2013).
[186] T. FRANCIS-NOËL & M. TURNER, CLEAR AND SIMPLE AS THE TRUTH (Princeton Univ. Press 1994).
[187] Jessica Strawser, *Alice Walker Offers Advice on Writing Conversation,* WRITER'S DIGEST (Aug. 31, 2010).
[188] KAHNEMAN, *supra* note 172.
[189] Conor Friedersdorf, *Why Clarence Thomas Uses Simple Words in His Opinions,* THE ATLANTIC (Feb. 20, 2013).
[190] CARDOZO, *supra* note 182.
[191] Futing Zou, Brive Kuhl, Sarah DuBrow & J. Benjamin Hutchinson, *Benefits of Spaced Learning*, 44 CELL REPS. (2025); David Price & Ting Wang, *The Effect of Spaced Repetition on Learning and Knowledge Transfer in a Large Cohort of Practicing Physicians*, 100(1) ACAD. MED. 94–102 (2025).
[192] RICHARD A. POSNER, REFLECTIONS ON JUDGING 276–77 (Harvard Univ. Press 2013).
[193] WILLIAM SHAKESPEARE, HAMLET (1603).
[194] Winston Churchill (1940).
[195] *Id.* (1942).
[196] *Id.* (1940).
[197] STAR WARS: THE EMPIRE STRIKES BACK (Twentieth Century Fox 1980).
[198] THE FEDERALIST NO. 51 (James Madison).
[199] Robert Jackson, Nuremberg Opening Statement (1945).
[200] John F. Kennedy, Inaugural Address (1961).
[201] Brown v. Allen, 344 U.S. 443 (1953) (J. Robert Jackson).
[202] Julius Caesar (47 B.C.).
[203] Kennedy, *supra* note 200.
[204] Gerber v. Hickman, 264 F.3d 882, 893 (9th Cir. 2001).

[205] Francis-Noël & Turner, *supra* note 186.
[206] DR. MARDY GROTHE, I NEVER METAPHOR I DIDN'T LIKE 304 (Harper Collins 2008).
[207] *In Justice Breyer's Opinion, A Footnote Has No Place*, N.Y. TIMES (July 28, 1995).
[208] N. Cowan, K. Donnell & J.S. Saults, *A List-Length Constraint on Incidental Item-to-Item Associations*, 20(6) PSYCHONOMIC BULL. & REV. 1253–8 (2013).
[209] N. Cowan, *The Magical Mystery Four: How Is Working Memory Capacity Limited, and Why?*, 19(1) CURRENT DIRECTIONS IN PSYCH. SCI. 51–57 (2010); Cowan, Donnell & Saults, *supra* note 208.
[210] Rebecca Johnson et al., *Are Two Spaces Better Than One? The Effect of Spacing Following Periods and Commas During Reading*, 80 ATTEN. PERCEPT. PSYCHOPHYS. 1504 (Aug. 2018).
[211] M.J.C. LOWRY, THE WORLD OF ALDUS MANUTIUS: BUSINESS AND SCHOLARSHIP IN RENAISSANCE VENICE (Cornell Press 1979).
[212] D. Marsh, *Oxford Commas? Let Common Sense Prevail*, THE GUARDIAN (July 4, 2011).
[213] June Casagrande, *A Word, Please: AP Softens on the Oxford Comma, but Its Rule Against the Punctuation Mark Can Make Sense*, L.A. TIMES (June 12, 2023).
[214] JILL BARTON, THE SUPREME GUIDE TO WRITING (Oxford Univ. Press 2024).
[215] LOWRY, *supra* note 211.
[216] KING, *supra* note 1.
[217] Martínez, Mollica & Gibson, *supra* note 53.
[218] Shaun Wallace et al., *Towards Individuated Reading Experiences: Different Fonts Increase Reading Speed for Different Individuals*, 29(4) ACM TRANSACTIONS ON COMPUTER–HUMAN INTERACTION, art. no. 38 (2022).
[219] A. Wolter, *The Psychology of Fonts & Their Impact on Conversions*, UNDULLIFY (July 12, 2022).
[220] Bryan Garner, *Judges on Briefing: A National Survey*, 8 SCRIBES J. LEGAL WRITING 10 (2001–2002).

[221] *Id.*
[222] KAHNEMAN, *supra* note 172, at 64.
[223] SCALIA & GARNER, *supra* note 184.
[224] FRANCOIS DE LA ROCHEFOUCAULD, REFLECTIONS; OR, SENTENCES AND MORAL MAXIMS, maxim 327 (1678).
[225] WILLIAM SHAKESPEARE, MACBETH, act 5, sc. 5, ll. 26-27.
[226] JANE AUSTEN, PRIDE AND PREJUDICE (V. Jones ed., Penguin Classics 2003).
[227] T. Shanahan & R. Lomax, *An Analysis and Comparison of Theoretical Models of the Reading–Writing Relationship*, 78(2) J. EDUC. PSYCH. 116–23 (1986) (finding reading provides a foundation for the acquisition of writing skills).
[228] Jill Fitzgerald & T. Shanahan, *Reading and Writing Relations and Their Development*, 35(1) EDUC. PSYCH. 39–50 (2000); Timothy Shanahan, *Relations Among Oral Language, Reading, and Writing Development*, *in* HANDBOOK OF WRITING RESEARCH 171–86 (2006).
[229] SCALIA & GARNER, *supra* note 184.
[230] Victor Feraru, *Jargon, Legalese and the Bluebook: My Conversation With Judge Richard A. Posner*, HUFFINGTON POST (Dec. 30, 2016).
[231] William Faulkner, Speech, Univ. of Miss. (April 1949).
[232] JAMES W. PENNEBAKER, THE SECRET LIFE OF PRONOUNS: WHAT OUR WORDS SAY ABOUT US (2011).
[233] Kuehl, *supra* note 180.
[234] KING, *supra* note 1.
[235] Scott Myers, *Writing Mantra: Writing is Rewriting*, MEDIUM (Nov. 26, 2021), https://gointothestory.blcklst.com/writing-mantra-writing-is-rewriting-e7fbe494adb.
[236] ERNEST HEMINGWAY, A MOVABLE FEAST (Scribner Classics 1964).
[237] Margaret Atwood, *Writing the Middle and Ending*, MASTERCLASS.COM (last visited Nov. 26, 2024).
[238] Patricia M. Wald, *19 Tips From 19 Years on the Appellate Bench*, 1 J. APPELLATE PRAC. & PROCESS 9 (Winter 1999).
[239] KING, *supra* note 1.

[240] Jacques Barzun, *English as She's Not Taught*, THE ATLANTIC (Dec. 1953).
[241] This quote is often attributed to Michelangelo, but I could not confirm that he was the original source.
[242] *Maya Angelou: An Interview*, THE PARIS REVIEW (1990).
[243] T. GOLDSTEIN & J. LIEBERMAN, THE LAWYERS GUIDE TO WRITING WELL 155 (Univ. of California Press 2002).
[244] THE BUDDHA, THE DHAMMAPADA, ch. 5 (The Fool).